Leading Professional Learning

Leading Professional Learning

Practical strategies for impact in schools

Helen Timperley, Fiona Ell,
Deidre Le Fevre, Kaye Twyford

Published in 2025 by Amba Press, Melbourne, Australia
www.ambapress.com.au

First published in 2020 by ACER Press, an imprint of
Australian Council for Educational Research Ltd

© Helen Timperley, Fiona Ell, Deidre Le Fevre, Kaye Twyford 2025

This book is copyright. All rights reserved. Except under the conditions described in the *Copyright Act 1968* of Australia and subsequent amendments, and any exceptions permitted under the current statutory licence scheme administered by Copyright Agency (www.copyright.com.au), no part of this publication may be reproduced, stored in a retrieval system, transmitted, broadcast or communicated in any form or by any means, optical, digital, electronic, mechanical, photocopying, recording or otherwise, without the written permission of the publisher.

Edited by Holly Proctor
Cover design, text design and typesetting by Shaun Jury
Cover image © Beliavskii Igor, used under license from Shutterstock.com

ISBN: 9781923569423 (pbk)
ISBN: 9781923569430 (ebk)

A catalogue record for this book is available from the National Library of Australia.

Contents

Preface	ix
INTRODUCTION The complexity of professional learning in schooling improvement	1
The complexity of professional learning	2
Principles for professional learning that respects complexity	4
Responding to complexity using inquiry	7
This book: How does it help?	9
Coherence and sustained focus	9
Creating a learning culture	10
Emotion, uncertainty and vulnerability	10
Evidence and evaluative thinking	10
Equity, bias and beliefs	11
Case studies	11
Conclusion	12
CHAPTER 1 Coherence and sustained focus	13
The challenge	13
The reason why this is a challenge	14
Leadership actions to address the challenge	16
Don't comply, own it	16
Commit to an explicit plan with evaluative probes	17
Keep the main thing the main thing	20
Seek 'vertical' coherence	22
Interrogate new imperatives	24
See patterns and make links	25
Don't stop until you get there	26
Conclusion	27
CHAPTER 2 Creating a learning culture	29
The challenge	29
The reason why this is a challenge	30
Leadership actions to address the challenge	32
Make the school culture visible	33
Intentionally create a learning culture	34

Tackle the tough stuff	36
Keep the focus on students	37
Engage everyone in genuine inquiry	38
Use the spiral of inquiry to develop and sustain a learning culture	40
Conclusion	42

CHAPTER 3 Emotion, uncertainty and vulnerability — 45

The challenge	45
The reason why this is a challenge	46
Leadership actions to address the challenge	49
Help others understand the role of emotion in professional learning	50
Understand, notice and reduce unnecessary uncertainty	51
Consider risk, not resistance	56
Support others to take risks	58
Understand how trust works	60
Expect and navigate emotion when using the spiral of inquiry	61
Conclusion	62

CHAPTER 4 Evidence and evaluative thinking — 63

The challenge	63
The reason why this is a challenge	64
Leadership actions to address the challenge	65
Get the evidence in order	65
Use evaluative thinking in decision making	69
Interpret the evidence together	70
Seek new forms of evidence	72
Link evidence of student learning with changes in teaching, leadership and organisational practices	73
Give it time and keep coming back to it	75
Conclusion	77

CHAPTER 5 Equity, bias and beliefs — 79

The challenge	79
The reason why this is a challenge	80
Leadership actions to address the challenge	82
Examine equity policies and systems	82
Develop knowledge of how unconscious bias works	84
Use inquiry and evidence to check for and challenge bias and inequity	86
Surface and process problematic biases and beliefs	88
Deprivatise practice	90
Take affirmative, strengths-based action	90
Conclusion	91

CHAPTER 6 Extended examples 93

CHAPTER 7 Bringing things together for impact 113

References 119

Preface

We have written this book for school leaders who are faced with the increasingly daunting task of leading their schools to become ever more responsive to the challenges of change. Every school leader knows that more is expected of them and that the challenges they face are becoming more complex. Schools are expected to engage and educate all students through to their late teens when many of these students would rather be somewhere else. While all parents want their children to succeed, how they define success, and their beliefs about how schools should work to achieve it, can be challenging as the student body becomes more culturally and linguistically diverse. School leaders are expected to be responsive to all of these challenges with their efforts impacting positively on teaching, learning and improved student outcomes.

As a result, schooling improvement and innovation permeate the educational landscape and there is no shortage of advice about how to achieve it. While it is true that if we keep doing the same thing we will get the same results, it is also true that there is much about current schooling that is effective and there are good reasons for doing things the way they are currently done. This tension between maintaining what is effective while changing what is less effective adds to the complexity of change. There is always a pull towards the status quo counteracting a push to do things differently.

Central to change and improvement are professional learning and development for leaders and teachers, and these form the primary focus of this book. Yet it is here that the tension between maintaining the status quo and doing things differently is most obvious. Most professional development conducted through courses and workshops does not result in sustained change (Timperley, Wilson, Barrar, & Fung, 2008). While the success rate of school-based, longer term professional learning is a little better, much of it suffers the same fate.

In this book we seek to highlight some of the challenges that school leaders face when leading professional learning and development in their schools as part of an improvement agenda. The book is not a comprehensive how-to guide, but rather a practical resource for school leaders to identify and address

some specific issues that we have found in our research and development work to almost inevitably accompany the learning and change process. These challenges include:
- developing coherence and a sustained focus
- creating a learning culture
- working with the emotional impact of change as both leaders and teachers face new vulnerabilities
- using evidence and thinking evaluatively about impact
- addressing issues of equity, unconscious bias and beliefs that may be getting in the way of addressing these difficult issues.

Some of these challenges will feel familiar because they are an integral part of the many frameworks and resources designed to help schools to engage with a learning and improvement agenda. For example, the National School Improvement Tool jointly developed by the Australian Council for Educational Research (ACER) and the Queensland Department of Education, Training and Employment (2012) refers to, among other things, an explicit improvement agenda, the analysis and discussion of data, a culture that promotes learning, an expert teaching team and effective pedagogical practices. Similarly, ACER's (2018) Principal Performance Improvement Tool includes leading the moral purpose, creating enabling conditions, leading strategic change and promoting improved teaching. This book is designed to complement these tools by unpacking the challenges involved in translating them into the practical reality of leading schools.

We also want to note that we rarely refer to the principal separately from other leaders because the work of learning and improvement is too difficult for any one person. While a principal may be instrumental in initiating and driving change, sustained learning and improvement must become a collective responsibility. By leaders, therefore, we mean those in any positional or informal leadership role with responsibility for promoting the professional learning or improvement agenda in schools.

At the same time, we do not want to imply that school leaders are solely responsible for the professional learning of their staff without the assistance of external expertise. Those with specialist knowledge can contribute to the process of promoting professional learning and change and contribute specific content knowledge in a particular area. We do want to be clear, however, about an assumption underpinning our approach to this book. This assumption is that leaders must take an active role in promoting professional learning and change in ways that cannot be left to external experts. It is the responsibility of school leaders rather than those external to a school, for example, to develop coherence and a sustained focus across the school and its learning culture. Our research has also shown that, when school leaders address the emotional impact of change, trust is deepened and change is more accepted by teachers.

The research on which this book is based extends over many years when we, as authors, have worked in separate projects and together. One of the earlier works was *Best evidence synthesis on professional learning and development* (Timperley et al., 2008). This work analysed over 90 available studies on the approaches to professional learning that impacted on student outcomes. The findings from this synthesis were applied in a project involving 300 schools with significant improvement in student outcomes as a result (Timperley & Parr, 2009).

More recently, we have engaged collaboratively in a five-year research and development project that took place alongside a nationwide professional learning initiative in New Zealand between 2011 and 2016, involving over 250 primary and secondary schools. There were two main strands to the work. One strand monitored the progress of students in the schools that engaged with the professional learning to assess its impact on student achievement in the focus areas of reading, writing and mathematics. The second strand focused on the processes that promoted leaders' and teachers' professional learning and development. Twice a year the research findings were fed back to the professional learning group, allowing for co-construction of knowledge and reciprocal sharing of information and ideas. This process meant that our research findings were always examined closely by those who would use them, so we were challenged to make them relevant and useful. From this work we have identified the recurring challenges school leaders face when developing their staff through a change process, why those specific challenges have arisen and how some leaders have successfully overcome them.

At the same time, we have engaged in extensive research and development work in Australian schools, education departments and offices over the last 10 years. Much of this work has focused specifically on the enactment of the spiral of inquiry, learning and action (Timperley, Kaser, & Halbert, 2014), and has been particularly instrumental in identifying and addressing the challenges that form the themes in this book.

INTRODUCTION

The complexity of professional learning in schooling improvement

Sustainable change, improvement in teaching practice and better outcomes for students have become central to the work of all school leaders. Expectations of leadership include becoming ever more responsive to the complex challenges presented by an increasingly diverse student body. It is now a truism that, as the world 'outside' of education changes, so must the world 'inside' of education with much of the responsibility for leading the change resting with school leaders.

Leading professional learning within schools is always central to the change process. Three of the five professional practices within the Australian Professional Standard for Principals (Australian Institute for Teaching and School Leadership [AITSL], 2015)—leading teaching and learning; developing self and others; and leading improvement, innovation and change—directly address this challenge. Similarly, the Australian Professional Standards for Teachers (AITSL, 2011) contain an expectation that teachers will identify and plan their professional learning needs, engage in professional learning with colleagues and improve practice, and apply professional learning and improve student learning. Indeed, in most Australian states and territories, teachers must demonstrate they have engaged in activities to meet these standards through attending a minimum number of hours of accredited professional learning programs and in a variety of other ways. In addition, progress through the stages of graduate, proficient, highly accomplished and lead teacher is typically dependent on the presentation of a portfolio of practice demonstrating, among other things, engagement in professional learning.

While descriptions of professional standards and practices can form an impetus for improvement, it is much easier to write about them than it is to use them to bring about sustained change that has an impact on students' learning, achievement and wellbeing. They do serve an important purpose in outlining expectations, but there is little evidence to support the idea that the promulgation of standards, descriptions of professional practice or participation in professional learning programs have much effect (Timperley, Wilson, Barrar, & Fung, 2007). One of the ongoing frustrations in education is that there is an expanding body of research knowledge, supported by the learning sciences, that identifies teaching practices that are likely to be more effective than others (for example, Hattie, 2015), yet few of them are put into practice with integrity despite the hours and dollars spent in promoting their implementation. Even when teachers engage in high-quality courses based on the best of research-informed practices, such as assessment for learning, the impact on student outcomes is typically limited (James, 2006). This is not because teachers are resistant to new ideas or do not want to change, but rather because it is very difficult to do so (Jensen, Sonneman, Roberts-Hull, & Hunter, 2016; Opfer & Pedder, 2011; Twyford, Le Fevre, & Timperley, 2017). In reality, the challenge leaders and teachers constantly face is to meet the needs of diverse learners in complex settings, interacting in unpredictable ways with an uncertain curriculum (Le Fevre, Timperley, & Ell, 2015). Many approaches to professional learning do not support them to do this well.

The complexity of professional learning

Leading a school is a complex business—not just complicated, complex. 'Complex' is a word often used when it is difficult to keep track of all the factors that are impacting on a situation and it is hard to make sense of what is happening. Complicated situations or objects are ones where there are lots of things happening but, given enough time or skill, the pieces can be separated out and put back together and they will work in the same way. An example is the motherboard of a computer—it looks like a jumble to a layperson, but it can be dismantled and reassembled by a skilled person. Taken apart, each part and what it does can be understood; it can be fixed, or the part replaced to improve the computer's functioning. It is complicated, rather than complex. Complex phenomena are different. They are characterised by interactions and interdependencies. They cannot be meaningfully dismantled in order to be understood. If they are taken apart, the pieces will not be enough to understand how the whole thing works. One thing does not necessarily lead to another in a complex system, so 'fixing' a part of the system can lead to unexpected consequences, or to no change at all. Cause and effect are not closely linked—things spiral in a complex system, rather than proceed in straight lines as they do in complicated systems (Cochran-Smith, Ell, Ludlow, Grudnoff, & Aitken, 2014; Opfer & Pedder, 2011).

Leaders of professional learning often apply thinking that would work for a complicated situation to what is actually a complex situation. They might bring a professional learning program into the school thinking that it will target the 'bit' of practice that 'needs fixing', and once done, student outcomes in that area will improve. It is assumed that making changes can be enacted in the same learning environments in which this practice was previously absent. This linear thinking (problem with maths — maths professional learning package — better maths) is very tempting, and prevalent in education, especially in policy circles. It denies the reality of experience, though; when staff engage with a professional learning program there will be a range of responses — some practices might change, some people might change a lot while others seem impervious and the changes may last in some learning environments or be short-lived in others. 'Interventions', such as workshops, courses and programs, are predicated on teacher learning being complicated, but teacher learning is complex. It is not surprising that most have little sustainable impact.

If we accept that schools and teacher learning are complex phenomena, rather than complicated phenomena, what does that mean for leading professional learning? First, practice, and change in practice, need to be considered holistically, as products of teachers' or leaders' beliefs, values, experiences and knowledge. Each aspect of practice is linked to all others, and to the practitioner's identity and values. Trying to change just one aspect of practice is difficult in these circumstances.

Second, context is significant in shaping practice. Context includes obvious factors, such as the students, school community and staff profile, as well as the impacts of broader policy frameworks, resourcing decisions and professional body regulations. Schools do not exist in isolation; they are part of a web of fundamentally interconnected parts that comprise the broader education and social systems, which impact what they can do and how they can do it. Importantly, context also includes the history of the complex system — past attempts at change, the school culture and the way things have been done before. All of these things are not just background to any professional learning initiative, they are integral to it.

Third, complex systems are dynamic, constantly changing entities and they change and evolve through interactions. The flow of information and communication in a system are its life blood and frequent, recurring interactions are the means by which new understandings and practices develop. This means that a complexity-informed approach to professional learning within schooling improvement needs to pay attention to interactions and the ways in which talking and sharing between leaders and colleagues occur.

Trying to lead professional learning in ways that have an implicit view of teacher learning as complicated will not lead to transformative and lasting change because schools, professional learning and school improvement are inherently complex phenomena and need to be treated as such.

Principles for professional learning that respects complexity

When addressing the challenges of change and improvement through professional learning using a complexity lens, the interplay of students, teachers, leaders, parents and the wider education system needs to be considered. These players and their intersections form the context and are integral to improvement efforts. Does the school have a strong professional learning orientation where the expectations of leaders, teachers, students and community are high? Or, as a leader, is this the learning culture you are trying to develop through the professional learning process? How do teachers interact with one another and with you as leaders? Is there an openness to take risks or does everyone play it safe?

Then there is the complexity of each participating educator. What are the previous experiences of individual leaders and teachers in this learning-and-change space? How are the beliefs, knowledge, biases and motivations likely to interact with the changes proposed?

This complexity can feel overwhelming and it is impossible to attend to each part because they are all interwoven. Change in any one area will have a ripple effect through others. What we suggest as a way forward is that leaders design professional learning experiences according to a set of principles that address complexity and are consistent with the research that underpins high-quality professional learning with impact. We then go on to describe an inquiry process that fits with these design principles.

One important principle concerns developing teacher agency to make a difference to their student learners (Hattie, 2015). Learning to do something differently and to value something different demands letting go of past habits and beliefs. Those offering professional learning programs and those promoting them, such as policymakers or school leaders, are often more convinced that changes to teachers' practice will be of sufficient benefit to themselves or their students to make the effort worthwhile than the participating teachers are (Twyford et al., 2017). The kind of passivity and compliance generated when others make decisions for teachers about what will best help their learners is the antithesis of developing teacher agency. Such agency is about teachers and leaders 'being able to express their professional commitment and responsibility to bringing about change in ... educational achievement and accept professional responsibility for the learning of their students' (Bishop, 2010, p. 1). They believe they can make a difference and take the actions to do so, rather than being reactive to, or passive within, a given situation.

Developing teacher agency to make a difference means focusing on students. The research is definitive on this issue. Little is likely to change for students unless addressing particular issues with student learning is the reason to engage in professional learning and addressing these issues forms the basis for assessing the impact of any change to practice (Hattie, 2015; Timperley, 2011). A superficially defined issue in relation to student learning, such as low achievement in literacy skills, is insufficient. The problem must be diagnosed in depth (for example: Is it a problem with vocabulary or limited understanding of communicative purposes?) and the contributing issues unpacked (for example: Is it primarily a problem of motivation or a combination of motivation and skills?). New practices are then designed to address the diagnosis and contributing issues. Professional learning programs or courses that carry teaching practice titles such as 'Feedback' or 'Formative assessment' typically focus on the teaching practice, rather than the student learning issue the practice is intended to address. While these practices can have high effect sizes when implemented well in research settings, there is no guarantee they will address the needs of any given teacher's diverse learners— not only because they are constantly interacting in unpredictable ways with an uncertain curriculum but also that the teachers themselves fit this description. A more holistic approach is more effective.

Professional learning must be supported by, and embedded in, a coherent learning culture focused on a few priority, student-focused goals if it is to make a difference (Jensen et al., 2016; Timperley et al., 2014). Complexity theory highlights the influence of the context on how a teacher teaches, their motivation to engage in new learning and their ability to change practice. This issue is central to the idea of embedding teacher professional learning within a schooling improvement context with a few priority goals on which everyone is focused. Many approaches to professional learning act as if the school is a collection of individual teachers each doing their own thing rather than an organisation with coherence where the context influences the thinking and actions of individuals who, in turn, influence the context.

Professional learning implies the development of new knowledge and skills. This principle means engaging deeply in new learning through multiple opportunities to learn and practise over time (Timperley, 2011). Because teaching is a practice, new learning about teaching can best be understood through practice. There will be times when the underpinning ideas are presented and discussed but, ultimately, the new learning needs to be supported in situ if it is to be enacted in the complexity of the practice context. The acquisition of new skills or knowledge cannot be considered additive, that is, simply building on what is already known. New ideas are likely to challenge existing beliefs, assumptions and biases because individuals bring a history of both learning and practice to a particular situation.

The final principle concerns the use of evidence. While many teachers believe they know what is going on for their learners, they rarely gather evidence systematically from the learners' perspectives and involve them in its interpretation. Nor do teachers use a range of evidence to assess the impact of any changes they make to their practice or use it to decide what to retain because it is working and what to change because it is not. Evidence is sometimes thought of in terms of the National Assessment Program–Literacy and Numeracy (NAPLAN) or final year examinations. This kind of evidence can provide an overall picture of a cohort but fails to give a detailed, just-in-time picture of student progress in the improvement process. The development of more detailed measures is essential to making good instructional decisions.

All these principles are dependent on working with others to discuss, dissect, and reintegrate ideas and evidence, and figure out how they impact on practice. Learning is essentially relational and social (Dumont, Istance, & Benavides, 2010). Our brains are primed for social interaction and the construction of individual knowledge occurs through negotiation and cooperation with others. These 'others' may include those with specialist expertise together with colleagues who are experiencing similar challenges. Leaders must also be among the 'others' to support the learning and change process in situ and to challenge when learning is limited or problematic assumptions are getting in the way. Leaders are essential to help situate the new learning in the school improvement process and ensure it is focused on students.

These principles together address the complexity of change. In the next section we describe how inquiry approaches to professional learning can weave the principles together in ways that have an impact and are supported by research evidence (Jensen et al., 2016; Timperley & Parr, 2009).

Responding to complexity using inquiry

There are different inquiry approaches promoted throughout Australia. Some of these are officially sanctioned while others are more locally based. Most have many features in common, with the main driver being to develop in leaders and teachers a genuine curiosity about what is going on for learners together with the agency and skills to make a difference. In order to illustrate how all the principles are enacted through an inquiry process, the spiral of inquiry, learning and action, based on the work of Timperley et al. (2014), is described here and illustrated in Figure A. The spiral is based on an extensive review of the literature (Timperley et al., 2007) and other research (for example, Timperley & Parr, 2009) and there are many networks of schools across Australia putting this inquiry framework into action. Given the constraints of space, we have limited this description to a brief overview, but a more elaborated version is described in Timperley et al. (2014). In addition, two extended case studies are provided in the final chapter of this book describing how one secondary and one primary school worked through the spiral, made some false starts, then met the challenges that arose.

In the spiral of inquiry, learning and action, during the scanning phase, a team of leaders and teachers, or a whole school, begin by engaging in an evidence-informed process designed to develop their curiosity about what is going on for their student learners in their academic learning, wellbeing and

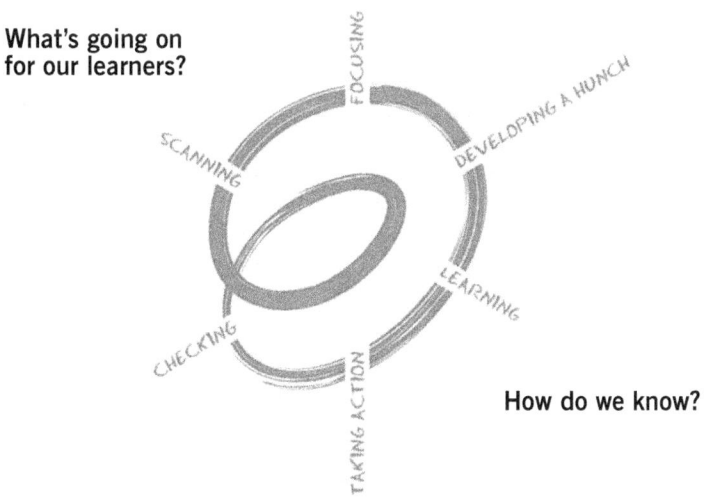

FIGURE A: Spiral of inquiry, learning and action.
Source: Timperley, H., Kaser, L., & Halbert, J. (2014). *A framework for transforming learning in schools: Innovation and the spiral of inquiry*. Seminar paper 234. Melbourne, VIC: Centre for Strategic Education. Reprinted with permission from the Centre for Strategic Education.

intellectual engagement. They do this by engaging with students, observing them and analysing their responses to academic tasks. While many teachers believe they know their learners well, it is rare that they sit down and ask them what is happening for them with genuine curiosity. Teachers invariably report surprises, particularly in the responses from those students who are struggling academically or socially. Involving students in both collecting the evidence, and more importantly, in the process of interpreting it, enhances their sense of agency in their own learning. After all, it is their learning that is at stake.

From this evidence and analysis, the team then focus on an area in which their students are experiencing difficulties that are impacting on their success, such as self-regulation of their learning or misunderstanding important concepts. This phase draws on the research literature to identify the areas of student learning that are most likely to lead to greater success. It is important to be tightly focused. Improving reading comprehension or vocabulary is more focused rather than reading more generically. A tight focus makes it more manageable for teachers to learn in sufficient depth to make a difference to their practice; they can observe progress in their students more quickly, which, in turn, helps to increase their motivation and commitment.

The next phase of 'developing a hunch' is rarely addressed in an inquiry process. It asks the team to establish hunches and consider how they might be contributing to the current situation. This phase is key to bringing to the surface those beliefs and assumptions that may be getting in the way of teachers changing their practice. It is central to addressing the complexity of the change process, and creating agency and motivation, to engage in new learning through identifying for themselves what it is they need to learn and change if they are to make a difference for those student learners they are particularly concerned about.

The phases of learning and taking action interact with one another. Usually some professional learning takes place outside of the teaching environment, but it needs to be supported in situ for deep learning and change to occur. The more this process is embedded in a coherent learning system across a school or faculty, such as well-led professional learning communities, the more successful the learning and change process is likely to be. The intellectual and practical demands required of this deep learning means that any one educator can be involved in only one area of learning at any given time and they need to continue their involvement for an extended period.

The final phase involves formal checking to find out if the new learning and changed practices are actually making enough of a difference to their students. This requires the collection of more evidence that parallels the evidence collected in the early phases of the spiral. An important purpose for engaging in the spiral is to develop an inquiry mindset of evaluative thinking so that educators are asking on a daily basis if their students are learning what they are supposed to be learning, more quickly and more deeply than they did before.

Although Figure A portrays the spiral as a series of phases, they are iterative and often overlap. 'What's going on for learners?' and 'How do we know?' are the two key questions that underpin and drive all the phases. Scanning is often based on hunches and hunches arise from the scanning evidence. Refocusing often follows when more sophisticated hunches are tested. New learning happens throughout the spiral, as does checking if the team are making enough of a difference to their student learners. And, of course, checking is not the end of the process but rather merges into another spiral and becomes the core business of leading, teaching and learning. When those involved develop an inquiry mindset, real change occurs with improvement plans realised and gains sustained.

This book: How does it help?

Although we have outlined inquiry as a way to tackle professional learning, inquiry and any other approach to professional learning designed as part of an improvement agenda risk similar challenges. Chapters 1 to 5 in this book identify some of these recurrent challenges, outlining the reasons they present as challenges when planning and implementing professional learning for impact. Each of these chapters then offers specific suggestions about how to meet the challenge. Consistent with the theme of complexity, the chapters intersect with one another and are not necessarily intended to be read in order because addressing one challenge has both intended and unintended consequences and a ripple effect on the whole. Linearity of cause and effect processes in professional learning rarely happens.

Coherence and sustained focus

The underlying theme of complexity explains why a book on leading professional learning identifies coherence and sustaining a focus for improvement as the first major challenge. 'Quick fixes' are tempting to look for because it is difficult for school leaders to sustain an improvement focus for sufficient time and in sufficient depth to reach the desired outcomes in a very crowded change agenda. There is always pressure to do more and, as a result, to do too much, too superficially, with little impact.

Creating a learning culture

The second challenge focuses on creating a learning culture throughout a school. Learning cultures are difficult to get a handle on, even more difficult to develop and often fragile in the longer term. Organisational changes, such as professional learning communities, are often introduced as ways to change the culture, but what happens within these communities is what counts, not the existence of such communities in themselves. Pseudo-inquiry can become the substitute for genuine inquiry (Le Fevre, Robinson, & Sinnema, 2015). Alternatively, a culture of 'niceness' can dominate where challenge and accountability all but disappear. A strong and sustained learning culture, focused on the moral imperative of making a difference for student learners, is essential for sustained change.

Emotion, uncertainty and vulnerability

The third challenge focuses on a typically neglected issue of teachers' emotions—their trust and vulnerability. Slow, ineffective or unsustainable change initiatives are often attributed to teachers resisting changing the way they do things. This is not necessarily the case (Twyford et al., 2017). Many teachers wish to change but feel unable to do so because they perceive it to be too risky and feel vulnerable through the change process, often as a result of past experiences. Understanding the role of emotions in the change process and ways to address them are the foundation of working productively and collaboratively.

Evidence and evaluative thinking

The fourth challenge about the use of evidence and evaluative thinking is one much more widely recognised but rarely addressed well. Genuine and disciplined inquiry in school improvement must be based on evidence—but what evidence? How can it be used? Often 'evidence' is shorthand for formal test results, or other sources that are perceived to be 'hard' or 'objective' evidence. While these have important purposes, schools have many sources of rich evidence that are not well used. The challenge of using evidence well is to identify what evidence is available and what more needs to be collected, analysed and interpreted to identify if things are on the right track. Without good evidence, improvement efforts can quickly become 'activity traps' with anecdotes substituting for rigorous information as described by Katz, Earl, and Ben Jafaar:

> Activity traps are those 'doings' that, while well-intentioned, are not truly needs-based and have the effect of diverting resources (both human and material) away from where they are most necessary (2009, p. 24).

Equity, bias and beliefs

The final challenge relates to issues of equity, bias and beliefs about teaching and learning. Many improvement efforts have an equity focus but it is becoming increasingly evident that teachers and leaders often base their judgements about teaching programs and student learning on perceptions that underestimate the reality of what some students are actually achieving or able to achieve (Meissel, Meyer, Yao, & Rubie-Davies, 2017). As a result, expectations are lowered for some groups of students and teaching programs reflect these expectations. These unconscious biases are particularly prevalent for students who come from cultures different from the professionals who teach them. These biases make equitable outcomes unlikely.

Case studies

We conclude the book with two case studies that integrate and illustrate the themes and how they might look in a real situation of a primary and secondary school. The cases are based on our research and consultancy work in Australia and highlight the circumstances under which the challenges discussed in the earlier chapters are likely to arise and how they might be addressed. Each case study tracks through a typical problematic and more productive start to the spiral of inquiry, learning and action.

The cases can be used in a variety of ways and can be read at any time. Some readers might want to start with them because they describe the whole of the spiral of inquiry, learning and action through a narrative illustrating the complexity but also demonstrating ways through it. Others will prefer to wait until they have read about a challenge and want to find out how that can be addressed in a more holistic way, which will be described in each chapter. The other choice is to wait until the end and read how it can all come together.

Throughout the book we have included quotes from school leaders and teachers from a range of schools. We have worked with these people through many different projects and have not identified them specifically, but have identified which type of school they come from to provide the context.

Conclusion

There is limited time and energy in schools. Professional learning and improvement work is difficult. Without a principled approach and clear direction, these activities may have the impact of taking time away from the central demands of the job and become 'activity traps' (Katz et al., 2009).

In order to avoid professional learning and schooling improvement efforts becoming activity traps, leaders of professional learning need to understand the complexity that is present in people, schools and learning and take a principled approach to making change. We intend this book to help improve student learning, achievement and wellbeing in ways that are effective, manageable and sustainable.

CHAPTER 1
Coherence and sustained focus

The challenge

Schools are very busy places. Leaders and teachers often feel as though they rush all day from one thing to another, dealing with emerging crises and responding to unexpected events. By the end of each school term, everyone is tired, stressed, frantic, worn out. Under these conditions it is a challenge to maintain coherence and a sustained focus on a particular improvement project. There seem to be so many competing, urgent demands that focusing on one thing is an indulgence that cannot be afforded. 'Quick fix' programs, packages, methods, books, internet resources, digital solutions and professional learning experiences abound, and it is tempting to use these to feel like you are doing something to move your school forward. In education, it is easy to get excited about the next book or the next resource in a search for answers. To slow down, look deeply into what is happening and work systematically through an improvement process may seem like an unattainable luxury and is challenging in a culture of busyness—yet it is essential to making real and sustained change that improves outcomes for learners (Bryk, Sebring, Allensworth, Luppescu, & Easton, 2010; Robinson, Bendikson, McNaughton, Wilson, & Zhu, 2017).

What is coherence? Developing coherence involves aligning the focus of improvement work across levels of the school. This means that the focus of the school improvement plan is in the policies, is in the goals for the school, is in planning done by departments or key learning areas or year groups, is in professional learning initiatives, is in teachers' personal goals, is communicated to the school community, and so on. The channeling of resources towards specific and unified goals also contributes to coherence.

Challenges to coherence typically come from two different directions. There may be tensions between school goals and priorities at state and federal levels that can derail school leaders' best intentions to create coherence. Sometimes these tensions also come from within the school itself as individuals and groups of teachers prefer to put their efforts into other priorities that they see as more relevant to their jobs.

The reason why this is a challenge

At all levels, from school leadership to student learning, education is a complex enterprise, as we outlined in the Introduction. Every layer is characterised by difficult problems, unexpected outcomes, and high-stakes decision making, all of which impact on one another. Leaders face multiple, and often competing, demands with responsibility for buildings, health and safety, curriculum, assessment, teachers, students, their families and the school's role in the community. Teachers also work under conditions of cognitive overload, making hundreds of decisions a day about how to respond to learners and their families. Under these circumstances, it is not surprising that leaders seek ways to simplify tasks and make their jobs more manageable.

Adding pressure to the sheer busyness of school is the significance of what schools do. Schools have a huge influence on the learners who attend them, for better or worse, and impact the families and communities that engage with them. Most educators are driven by the moral imperative of educating students—you are not making useful widgets, you are influencing the course of people's lives. Inequitable outcomes from education sharpen this moral imperative. An ongoing imperative is to work in ways that combat systemic disadvantage and marginalisation. Pushing against powerful social forces like these is tiring and difficult.

Against this backdrop of constant demands on brain space and energy, and the high-stakes nature of the work, it is little wonder that beginning and sustaining serious schooling improvement work is challenging. The demands and the significance of school do not just form a backdrop to improvement work. They must become part of the substance of it, which means that both the conditions in which improvement work occurs, and the work itself, are inherently challenging. By its nature, improvement is recursive, uneven, frequently meets obstacles and sometimes cannot be distinguished from the day-to-day busyness of schools. The times when focus and coherence are hardest to maintain are when they are most needed to keep momentum and to make change.

Things in schools are the way they are for a raft of historical, pragmatic, cultural and personal reasons. Anything focused on as needing change or improvement is currently being maintained by current beliefs and practices at student, teacher and leader (and sometimes community) levels. If teachers are teaching through direct instruction for every lesson, and you wish to change this, then it is important to realise that the teachers' behaviour is shaped by many different pressures. These include the students' responses, the teachers' confidence, competence and knowledge of alternatives and the conditions set by the structures of the school (perhaps they are having to test students every six weeks and find they cannot get through the curriculum unless they teach in this way). Leaders sometimes see improvement and change as having to occur in classrooms, without realising that school structures and processes shape what happens in classrooms. When and how teachers meet, how long learning sessions are, interruptions to the timetable, reporting requirements, appraisal processes and the tacit messages sent about what is valued in the school all influence teachers' work. Coherence and sustained focus cannot be achieved without looking at all the layers in a school.

Teachers' approaches may also be shaped by underlying beliefs about their learners (for example: 'They are not able to behave well enough for group work', 'They can't learn it unless I tell them', 'They don't have the independent skills to engage with these ideas'). These beliefs are powerful maintainers of behaviour. Working through these underlying issues is uncomfortable and time-consuming, making it tempting to reach for a professional development package or program (such as project-based learning, play-based learning or teaching through problem solving) instead of deep inquiry into what is happening and why, as described in the spiral of inquiry (Timperley et al., 2014) in the Introduction. Grabbing new and appealing ideas is understandable but it works against coherence and sustained focus, which will, in the end, yield more sustainable change. As one school principal told us:

> *Before we engaged in deep inquiry, we were trying everything. What we were actually doing was trying to solve the problem [of low literacy achievement] without knowing what the problem really was.*
>
> Principal, F–6 school

Two other forces can also work against coherence. One comes from 'above' in the form of compliance requirements and new policy initiatives imposing a layer of 'must dos'. The other originates from the genuine enthusiasm of teachers who want to make a difference and are eager to engage in new ways of doing things. 'Initiativitis' is a common education illness (Bryk et al., 2010) but the research is very clear: the more schools try to do in their improvement initiatives the less they achieve (Robinson, McNaughton, & Timperley, 2011). Schools are a very challenging context in which to create and maintain coherence and establish a sustained focus. It is something that everyone struggles with.

Leadership actions to address the challenge

The leadership actions outlined next are designed to help you to develop greater coherence in your professional learning and improvement efforts given the challenges we have identified. They are not a 'quick fix' or an 'easy answer' because there are none, but they do outline a systematic process to assist you to navigate through the complexity of the noise of schools' busy environments in ways that help to keep your improvement efforts on track.

Don't comply, own it

In order to build coherence and maintain focus, buy-in and commitment from staff, students and the school community are essential. This means that the focus of the work needs to be seen as worthwhile and aligned with valued outcomes. It needs to be something that people want to work on because they believe it will make a much-needed difference. This kind of buy-in is rarely achieved if compliance with external requirements is the main motivation for the work.

For leaders, compliance can take two forms: complying with a goal or idea that has been externally mandated or complying with a process that has been similarly mandated. In both cases it is difficult to build enthusiasm and motivation if questions like 'What are we supposed to do?' and 'When do we have to do it by?' predominate.

Initiatives by state authorities and others are usually founded on strong research, often arrive with resources and support materials, and so should not be rejected out-of-hand just because they are mandated. A synthesis of the evidence related to professional learning and development (Timperley et al., 2007) found that coherence between state, school and teacher goals often had a higher impact on student learning than locally based initiatives. This does not mean, however, that leaders ought to simply adopt the state's agenda. Rather, it means that aspects of this agenda are to be considered in relation to coherence, with leaders asking, 'How does this state initiative fit with our current improvement agenda?', 'Will it disperse or focus our energies?', 'Is this the right time in view of our other commitments?' and 'What parts of this actually align with our goals?'

The same mantra needs to guide teachers' commitment. They often feel they are complying with the leaders' improvement agenda. Teachers also need to 'own' it through being involved from the beginning about the evidence underpinning the choices made about the process.

Commit to an explicit plan with evaluative probes

Schools with explicit plans to improve are more likely to do so (Robinson et al., 2017). Planning tools and formats abound. What is important is that the plan has very specific information that includes who, what, when, where and how, with regular evaluative probes to monitor progress in leadership, teaching and learning built into the plan to assess progress.

Many plans are more like a wishlist than a working document that has been designed to achieve specific outcomes. An explicit and careful plan is underpinned by the beliefs of a school community that particular actions will result in improvement in particular outcomes for students. The process of identifying these beliefs needs to engage those responsible for implementing the plan (usually the teachers) and those affected by it (usually parents and/or students). Their engagement helps to identify what needs to be addressed and develops commitment and ownership. Many school leaders are disappointed that teachers show resistance or do not engage fully with an improvement agenda. This is predictable if they are not involved in identifying what needs to change and what support is needed to implement it. One principal, new to a school, explained:

> *Coming in here I felt like I just had the best plan for them—I'm going to get them through this, and we are going to do this and this is going to be great. That plan is still sitting there in that blue folder.*
>
> *Principal, P–8 school*

If plans are to make a difference to student learning, they must have this learning as the goal with everything else shaped around it. They need to start with the current profiles of student learning, engagement, motivation and wellbeing that are to be the focus for improvement, then specify, in some detail, the profiles for the student characteristics that are the intended outcome. This specification allows that progress towards meeting the goals to be monitored.

Most plans have professional development for teachers as the main way to address student learning needs but are rarely specific about issues with the current learning environments, teacher attitudes or skills that are to be the focus of change. If leaders have some concerns about these, they rarely share them with teachers. In the same way, the anticipated changes need to be specific. Ask yourself and your team, 'Is there agreement on how we want students to learn differently?' 'Is there agreement on the kinds of changes needed in the teaching–learning environment?' This specificity allows progress to be measured in both teaching and learning. In the absence of this specificity, inputs (for example, hours attended) become substituted for actual changes in practice.

Plans are often monitored on an annual basis. This is far too long to wait to find out if things are changing in leadership, learning environments and outcomes for learners. Regularly occurring evaluative probes (Earl & Timperley, 2016) need to be identified as part of the plan so that the question, 'Are we on track to reach our goal?' can be answered at least once a term. One kind of probe needs to focus on activities ('Are the planned activities actually happening?') and another on outcomes ('Are the shifts in leadership and teaching practice, together with outcomes for students, actually happening?'). Probes might take the form of key questions discussed at a staff meeting, with evidence brought along to back up ideas, or they could be observations of teacher practice, checks with students about their experience and whether it has changed, or parent responses that provide feedback on changes.

Sometimes these more extended plans are referred to as a theory for improvement because they contain more information than is typical of an annual plan and are more revealing of a school's reasoning. Theories for improvement do not stay static for a year but, at each review point (at least once a term), the next steps in the plan are adjusted according to previous progress. In this way they become working documents with all those involved helping to design the next term's work. Box 1.1 has a tool for evaluating the robustness of your plan and your evaluative probes. This tool asks you to assess the quality of your improvement plans against the criteria for a well-developed theory for improvement.

If you find there are gaps in your evidence about current student outcomes, don't delay the planning process. Rather, include ways to find out about the current situation as part of your plan or you might never get started.

A plan, or theory for improvement, that contains this level of information, as well as being specific about who will do what, by when, and with what resources, is a significant help in maintaining coherence and focus. The thinking that goes into this kind of planning works against being distracted, with all suggestions for new activities being assessed for coherence with the plan.

BOX 1.1
Evaluating a theory for improvement

Consider your current plan for improvement. Identify which of these criteria are strong in your plan and which might need to be strengthened to form a stronger theory for improvement.

Criteria for a theory for improvement	Rating 1–5 where: 1= absent 5= well developed	What next?
1. Longer term outcomes for your learners' achievement and specific targets for each term		
2. The current situation in relation to those targets for learners so you can identify the gaps		
3. The qualities of current learning environments and professional practices that are impacting on current achievement		
4. The qualities of new learning environments and professional practices you think will make a difference		
5. Proposed activities to change the learning environments to bring them closer to those you believe will help to reach the targets—usually staged because some things need to be in place before other things can happen		
6. A monitoring plan (evaluative probes) to identify if the activities in your theory for improvement are actually taking place and are resulting in progress towards your learner-related targets		

A principal, new to a school, explains what was happening when she arrived:

> *There were lots of initiatives in our school that meant we didn't have a focus; we had an annual plan but we didn't have a leadership team that was focused on the plan or on school improvement—it was based on units and centres in the school. Nobody could say what the plan was. So what's going on for us now is that we just don't know where we are heading.*
>
> Principal, K–8 school

Developing plans and theories of improvement, ideally, is a shared task. Who takes part will depend on the context but, generally, the more people who are involved, the greater the understanding and buy-in to the aims and goals.

Ideally, one version should be reduced to a 'plan on a page' so it can be readily displayed and referred to regularly during all schooling improvement and planning activities, with two questions constantly being asked: 'Are we on track?' and 'What do we need to adjust?' This can also help parents, governors, departmental advisors and other interested parties understand why you are saying 'No' to the next great idea and how you are creating coherence in your improvement efforts.

Keep the main thing the main thing

A critical mantra for building coherence and maintaining focus is 'keep the main thing the main thing'. Every challenge in schools is multi-causal and interdependent as described in the Introduction. For example, a challenge with students' progress in reading in a primary school might be the result of low teacher expectations, insufficient time given to reading instruction, teachers not knowing enough about how reading develops, insufficient resources to support reading, a shift to digital media reducing sustained engagement with print, low support of reading practice by families or students not seeing the relevance of reading to their lives. All of these things are interrelated: the students' attitudes will arise in part from their teachers' expectations and a lack of engaging resources, the teachers' expectations are fuelled by their inadequate knowledge of what reading progress should look like and so on. To make improvements to complex challenges, it is important to go deeply into one part of them at a time, recognising that each part is fundamentally connected to the others and learning how to transfer new knowledge and ways of working to other parts of the challenge (Timperley et al., 2014).

As you get deeper into the issues, however, it is easy to be distracted and end up in 'activity traps' (Katz et al., 2009) where everyone is busy doing things, but they are not impacting the planned focus or are trying to 'fire fight' all the things that arise. At these times, it is important to 'keep the main thing the main thing' and come back to the focus.

Another principal reflected on engaging with a strategic planning process with her staff, where she realised the importance of selecting a focus and looking at it in depth:

> *I will never forget the day where we had to do the school improvement plan. If you try and improve all things for all people, all the time, nothing actually happens.*
>
> Principal, K–12 school

In a broad sense, focusing on 'keeping the main thing the main thing' shapes choices about what is given attention and energy. When faced with multiple competing demands, returning to the agreed focus for improvement can help make decisions that build coherence: 'Yes, a new professional learning initiative looks interesting, but we are "keeping the main thing the main thing"'. If you do this, then choices will develop coherence and sharpen the focus, rather than becoming a distraction. One counter-intuitive distraction, or challenge to keeping focus, involves enthusiastic teachers who are wanting to try new things and make changes. While their enthusiasm can be fuel for school-wide improvement, their energy needs to be channelled into 'keeping the main thing the main thing' and using their creativity and ideas to work on the shared goals of the school. A principal explains how 'stars' can work against coherence and sustained focus:

> *In fairness to the teachers, some have done things differently, and individual classes have done some fabulous stuff. So individually we've been okay but collectively we haven't—and the teachers who are going ahead seem to ignore the others, and the ones that haven't changed just see it as too hard to do what the go-ahead teachers are doing, so for students, it's uneven.*
>
> Principal, K–12 school

'Keeping the main thing the main thing' as a strategy for developing coherence is only powerful if the 'main thing' is worthwhile. It should always be a student learning or wellbeing challenge. Essentially, 'keeping the main thing the main thing' reminds everyone that actions should be centred on students' needs and aspirations. In schools there are myriad 'layers' surrounding students and student outcomes and, inevitably, leaders need to intervene in those layers in order to make improvements for students. For example, a leader might decide to look at changing the way teachers approach teaching writing in order to improve students' writing outcomes. The 'main thing' is not the teachers' practice, but the students' outcomes, even though the actions to achieve the outcomes are at the level of the teachers' practice. The key here is to keep coming back to the students' learning to evaluate if changes in teaching practice are having the desired impact on students, rather than asking the question, 'Have the teachers changed their practice?' The actions are all in the service of the 'main thing': the experiences of students, their learning and wellbeing.

Seek 'vertical' coherence

Robinson et al. (2017) analysed the organisational coherence of five secondary schools that had different patterns of student achievement. In schools where achievement was improving, they found higher levels of coherence, and in particular the 'degree to which the[ir] goals were vertically integrated' (Robinson et al., 2017, p. 21). Vertical coherence refers to having all levels of the school working towards the same explicit goals, using the same theory for improvement.

Vertical coherence involves linking activity at all levels (senior leadership, middle leadership, teachers in their classrooms, students, community) to the same goals in explicit ways. In schools where teachers can explain what the school improvement goals are and how their professional learning and classroom practice links to those goals, improvement is more likely to occur. Vertical coherence requires clarity about how the school goals will be achieved through activity in different parts of the school (for example, through resourcing, timetabling, changes to classroom practice, changes in staff meeting formats, changes in professional learning opportunities). Gaining this clarity involves discussing the goals and the evidence underpinning them with all those affected and, through this process, gaining greater buy-in to, and understanding of, the goals themselves.

Clear and accessible plans, mentioned previously, are key tools in establishing vertical coherence. Frequent communication, 'check ins' and clarity from leaders will all help to build coherence as the plans are enacted.

When people (staff, families and students) can see that the plan is being put into effect seriously, with proper resourcing and evaluation, feelings of commitment and trust build up. Seeking vertical coherence helps improve outcomes for learners, and it can also help with building a collaborative learning culture and gaining trust. Figure 1.1 illustrates this vertical coherence and the ideas in the previous section on keeping the main thing as the main thing. Student learning and wellbeing are at the centre. Teacher learning is focused on improving outcomes for students, with leader learning focused on developing the knowledge and skills to work with teachers to improve outcomes for learners. Ideally, policy learning in the outside circle is focused on promoting conditions for school improvement because, as mentioned earlier, coherence with policy priorities has added benefit. The concentric circles represent the whole of the work of each group, with the improvement agenda focused in the 'wedge'. Deep learning is transferrable learning (Pellegrino & Hilton, 2012), which means that opportunities to learn deeply in the 'wedge' lead to transfer of professional learning to other aspects of teachers' work, thus creating a more comprehensive, but still focused, improvement agenda over time.

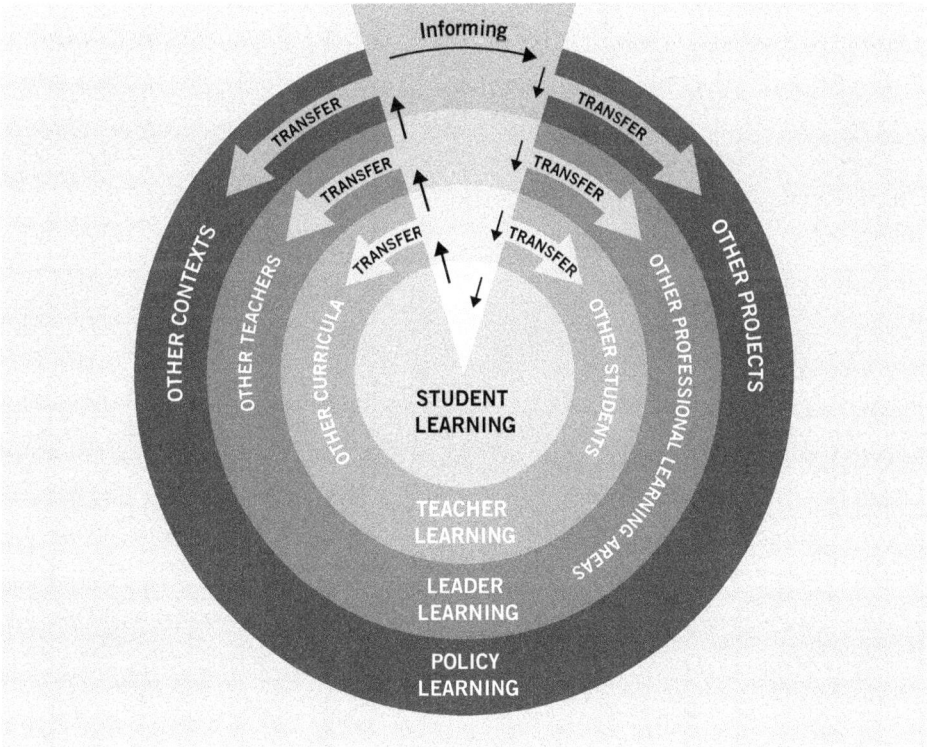

FIGURE 1.1: Vertical coherence for focused learning

Interrogate new imperatives

Once a clear plan and theory for improvement are in place, and the idea of keeping the main thing as the main thing is established, a threat to coherence and focus is the arrival of new imperatives, from either inside or outside the school. Major events, community concerns, new policies or curricula, new software or data gathering and reporting requirements, loss of staff, or mandated professional learning initiatives are examples of the inevitable challenges faced by schools that can mitigate against coherence and sustained focus. Some of these things can be ignored, or put on the 'back burner', tackled by limited numbers of people or turned down politely—but some cannot. The key skill here is discerning which things are essential, useful or necessary and which are distractions—and then working out how the necessary disruptions fit into the overall plan. This means interrogating new imperatives for their coherence with your improvement agenda, rather than unquestioningly accepting them. The tool in Box 1.2 is designed to help with this interrogation.

BOX 1.2
Interrogating new initiatives

When you, or someone else in the school is developing your annual plan or considering taking on something new, use this protocol to think carefully about how new things fit with what you are doing currently.

Do we have to do this? For whom would we be doing this?	Why do we/don't we have to do it?
Who will benefit if we do this?	Who will be disadvantaged if we do this?
Does any aspect of this fit with our goals and plans? How?	If we have to do it, but it doesn't fit, what's the least disruptive way to do it?
Can this be done in a way that 'keeps the main thing the main thing' and enhances what we are trying to do?	If it seems really important and beneficial, but it doesn't fit with our plan, why is that? What was our plan missing that this has picked up on? Does the plan need to change?
Is there a better time to do this? Or a better way to achieve the same aim that fits with our goals and plans?	If we decide to do it, what does that mean for us and our colleagues/students/school community? Are we going to put something else aside to do this or do we have the capacity to do it?

See patterns and make links

A key skill in building coherence and sustained focus is being able to see patterns and make links between things. Sometimes two things have different names, brands or curriculum contexts but are, in essence, the same thing—and recognising and naming this explicitly builds coherence. For example, many pedagogical recommendations and professional learning initiatives are predicated on the idea of getting to know the students' strengths and needs and using this knowledge to provide timely and useful feedback on students' learning. This may involve learning about progressions in student learning in a particular curriculum area, diagnostic tasks or tests and ways to provide feedback to students that build useful mindsets and skills. The initiatives may have different names, or be in different subject areas, but the key messages form a pattern. By linking them up, a coherent picture emerges where teachers are all working on the same powerful pedagogical idea, even if it is in different subject matter contexts. Most importantly, students get consistent messages across classes in ways that shape their approach to learning.

Leaders have an important role to play in discerning these patterns and communicating them to others in ways that build a sense of 'connectedness' and coherence. For people who are working in other layers of the organisation, the view afforded to leaders is often obscured. What seems coherent from a leadership perspective might not seem so to teachers or students. Finding regular ways to communicate about how things are 'joined up' helps to build coherence among everyone and enhances trust.

Identifying patterns and links means working at the level of deep ideas, sometimes called powerful ideas, underlying concepts or principles. These fundamental concepts underpin a wide variety of practices—but it is the underlying ideas that are important, rather than the particular ways in which they are expressed in context. Trying to work at the level of deep or powerful ideas and gain coherence around these ideas—rather than at uniformity of practice—will have greater impact on student learning outcomes. Coherence does not mean that everyone does the same thing; it means that everything that people do is in the service of the same big ideas.

This idea of patterns can also apply to the change process itself. In a study of 300 schools in New Zealand that used an inquiry approach, those that sustained their improvements in teaching practices and student learning once the external professional development was withdrawn, asked themselves, 'What did we learn in this improvement focus approach that we can use to inform the next improvement focus and approach?' Those that were less successful in sustaining their improvements in teaching practices or student learning treated their improvement foci as disconnected from one another. 'We have done this focus, now what is our next focus?' (Timperley & Parr, 2009). The tool in Box 1.3 can help identify the links between previous foci and new foci.

BOX 1.3
Making Links Tool

Think about what you are learning in your current focus. The prompts in the left-hand column are indicative suggestions—add any more headings you need for your context in order to summarise what you have learned. Then think about which aspects of your learning can be applied to the next focus. What links can be made?

Possible focus areas	What we have learned in our current focus	What we can apply to the next focus
Approach to change process		
Organisational changes		
Leadership practices		
Assessment practices		
Teaching practices		
Expectations of students		
Student behaviours (e.g. setting learning goals)		

Don't stop until you get there

The calendar-year nature of schools, where students pass through and each year the teachers work with different students, often leads to 'calendar-year thinking': 'This year we are doing maths', 'Last year we did reading', 'This year we are doing problem solving' and so on. When the end of the school year comes, that chapter is closed and a new one begins in the following year.

This approach mitigates against coherence and sustained focus. When goals have not been met when the year ends, the strong temptation is to begin the new year with a blank slate. Working from year to year often means spending time defining challenges, looking at evidence, and beginning to take action then running out of time to evaluate the impact of these actions and making evidence-based change. Thinking in longer cycles than a year (or shorter cycles for more restricted challenges) is imperative to increase the ability to build coherence and sustain focus, and thus to improve student outcomes. Revisiting and revising goals and your theory for improvement annually is important—and should be done with evidence in hand—but keeping going until you get there is important for making lasting improvements.

Conclusion

Coherence and sustained focus have been found to be associated with improved outcomes for learners in a range of settings (Bryk et al., 2010; Robinson et al., 2017). In addition, having a shared, sustained focus can build a collaborative culture and increase trust as people realise that what they are being asked to do is aligned with worthwhile outcomes and being properly resourced and evaluated. Creating coherence and focus in busy schools (which have multiple goals and many moving parts) is a serious challenge for leaders—however, the research evidence is strong that coherence and focus are worth the energy and commitment they take to develop. Using tools such as clear plans that are owned by all, regular communication about direction, and monitoring if it is all on track, will help bring a strategic focus to the busyness of school life and build coherence across the school.

CHAPTER 2
Creating a learning culture

The challenge

Every school has a culture, often referred to as an organisational culture. This culture can work for, or against, developing a learning culture.

A school's organisational culture is made up of the norms, attitudes, values, traditions and myths that are at the very core of the organisation. This culture is powerful because it influences the way people think, what they value and what they do. Often people are unaware of how much they are influenced by the culture of the school in which they work. Promoting powerful professional learning in schools requires that leaders create an organisational culture that supports the development of a learning culture.

What is a learning culture? A learning culture prioritises learning for everyone in the school. In a learning culture, people know that learning matters and is valued and celebrated. Essentially, it is a set of values and practices that supports individuals, groups and, indeed, the entire organisation or school in continuous learning and improvement. Resources are channelled towards supporting the learning of everyone in the school in all roles (students, teachers, leaders, community). It is clear that everyone is a learner, and this is communicated transparently, rather than relying on unwritten norms, expectations and expected ways of working. It has a positive impact on the learning, achievement and wellbeing of students, staff and leaders within a school, and the community of which it is part.

Ideally, the organisational culture supports a learning culture, but this is not always the case. At its worst, it actually inhibits the existence of a learning culture. For example, a school culture that is fiercely driven by traditional, individualist and competitive ways of doing things, makes it difficult for teachers to be innovative, to collaborate and try new approaches to teaching or to even have a vision of how things could be different. Changing existing school cultures so they can support learning cultures is within the power of school leaders—they have the power to lead such changes by understanding the impact of the school culture and intentionally ensure it supports a learning culture.

The reason why this is a challenge

A school's organisational culture is not always apparent; organisational culture can be difficult to identify and its impact can be hard to appreciate. Assumptions and beliefs often operate unconsciously; they can be invisible and yet are powerful because they define, in a basic 'taken-for-granted' fashion, the way people feel, think and act (Schein, 2017). Organisational cultures can almost take on a life of their own; they tend to reproduce themselves over time and outlast the individuals who pass through a school.

The pervasive nature of organisational cultures partly explains why, in the past, large-scale reform has often failed. These reforms have typically focused primarily on the development of innovations and not paid enough attention to the cultures in which innovations are enacted. A larger culture that does not support a learning culture is problematic. Challenges to the traditions and norms that support problematic cultures often become undiscussable in the professional spaces where they need to be addressed. For example, a group of teachers may be actively identifying issues in student engagement and working together to understand and address these. However, in the larger culture of the school there could be a sense that business as usual is fine and any interruption to this is undesirable. Teachers then live with the tension of trying to bring about improvement within a larger culture in which they are not in positions of power. As a result, the tensions are talked about in the parking lot, the restrooms or the dinner table at home (Barth, 2002) and so remain in place and unresolved.

Rather than challenge the deeper cultural norms, a frequent approach to improvement is to focus on structural changes in an effort to create a learning culture. For example, many states in Australia have created expectations and provided time for teachers to participate in professional learning communities. The intention is for them to work collaboratively to improve their teaching and student learning. Although well intentioned, it has become repeatedly apparent that these structural changes are not sufficient to bring about the desired improvement in learning for students or the practices of those responsible for educating them. Why? Because they fail to address the needed cultural change. What matters is how teachers and leaders feel, think and act in these professional learning communities. What teachers focus on and how they discuss problems of practice also matters. Is it safe to expose vulnerabilities, challenge one another and take risks? Research by DuFour (2011) indicates that it is rare for teachers to act in this way, they are rather more likely to engage in a culture of 'niceness' where everyone accepts what anyone says — are supportive rather than challenging of one another and avoid the tough issues. These norms jeopardise opportunities for real learning and changing outcomes.

Some Australian states promote a collaborative inquiry approach as the core process underpinning learning in professional learning communities. The inquiry process adds to the challenges identified earlier for collaboration, in particular, for ensuring that conditions are created for genuine inquiry driven by curiosity. Genuine inquiry asks educators to seek new insights into what is happening for learners, how the professionals might be contributing to the challenges identified, to experiment with possible innovative solutions and evaluate their impact.

At times, inquiry processes more closely resemble pseudo-inquiry (Le Fevre et al., 2014). Pseudo-inquiry features solutions that are already identified and asks questions to which some of the participants believe they already have an answer. Under these circumstances, the purpose of the 'inquiry' is to lead others to come up with the same answer. It is challenging to identify and change these types of 'pseudo-inquiry' patterns as they are very common both in schools and in life beyond. For example, a large primary school that was engaging with the spiral of inquiry (see the Introduction) had already had some success at lifting literacy results and the leadership team were keen to do the same for mathematics. They felt that the two key elements of the literacy initiative — having a shared lesson structure and a shared planning format — should be implemented in mathematics. They did not want to 'tell' the teachers what they wanted and the team's beliefs hampered their deep engagement with the scanning and focusing phases of the spiral of inquiry. This pseudo-inquiry led to a situation where, after a year, despite a stated focus on problem solving, the only observable change was a new shared planning format. This principal's summary illustrates this issue:

> *I was a bit indifferent to the inquiry process. We sort of had our own thoughts about what we were going to do and what we were going to be. So, it was more about how are we going to use this process to get to where we wanted to go. So, it was a bit of a look-see from my end. I was quite keen for our people to gather evidence and to be able to come together.*

> *Then I was pleased to see that the investigations ended up where we were hoping it would.*
>
> Principal, K–6 school

This example highlights another challenge in creating a learning culture. At times, leaders hold expectations that teachers need to change their thinking and practice through collaboration and inquiry but do not see themselves as central to the process. They do not realise that the cultural change underpinning effective collaboration and inquiry in professional learning communities requires systemic changes at all levels in the school. Leaders need to lead differently if teachers are to collaborate and learn how to teach differently. Leaders may not recognise that they need to engage in ongoing professional learning for their own practice in addition to providing professional learning for teachers. Developing a coherent learning culture that keeps students as the main focus requires everyone to be involved.

A major challenge for leaders is that they do not necessarily 'see' the organisational culture and how it impacts on teacher collaboration, professional learning and change. In the same way, they may not see themselves as the people who need to change in order to create an organisational culture that supports a learning culture across the school. Rather, they take a stance that 'everyone but me' needs to change with intentions and actions directed at others rather than themselves. For change to impact organisational norms, these actions need to be consistent across the school.

Despite these difficulties, establishing a learning culture can be done. Learning cultures enable people to feel safe to take risks and provide access to necessary knowledge and skills. Establishing and maintaining a strong and supportive learning culture throughout a school is essential to its improvement.

Leadership actions to address the challenge

A learning culture encourages and supports students, teachers and leaders throughout the school to continually learn and thrive. At an organisational level, a learning culture supports the school to learn as a whole by maintaining a trajectory of continuous improvement. Creating and sustaining a learning culture is therefore an important part of the work of leading powerful professional learning for the purposes of schooling improvement. The six leadership actions outlined here are high-leverage starting points for building a learning culture. Although these actions are listed separately, building this culture will require a combination of actions, and all schools will be in a different place with these ideas, so think carefully about your context as you consider what you need to do.

Make the school culture visible

School culture often operates beyond our awareness. It is important, however, to identify what the school culture feels like, what the culture expects of those who are part of the community and what the culture enables for those in the community. This understanding can explain why things happen the way they do, why people feel the way they do and why plans do not turn out in expected ways.

One way of thinking about making the school culture visible is to think of an iceberg. The smallest section of the iceberg is the part that is above the water and easily visible; this is what is seen readily yet does not constitute the bulk of the iceberg. Most of it is, in fact, below the water, out of sight, yet it constitutes a huge hazard to a ship that might venture too close. With school culture there are the daily interactions and routines, the ways of reacting and the artifacts that are easy to see. But what is beneath these? What is driving these more visible everyday aspects of the school? Making this school culture visible is an important step in the work of creating a school that has a learning culture. A suggested way to do this is outlined in Box 2.1.

BOX 2.1
School Culture Tool

Engage staff (at all levels and in all roles) in a deliberate discussion of the school's culture, using the iceberg metaphor to delve into what lies underneath daily actions and assumptions. The questions get more challenging as you go down the list.

- If someone just walked into our school, what would they notice that is unique to us?
- How do we support professional learning in this school?
- What gets in the way of us learning to do things differently?
- What are the taken-for-granted values and beliefs that influence 'the way we do things around here'?
- What are the non-discussables and the non-negotiables in our school?
- What does 'business as usual' look like?
- What does this culture foster and what does it send underground that stops some things happening that we want to happen?
- What is easy to get done and what is hard to get done?

The school culture is created and sustained by all those in a school, so the work of identifying a school culture needs to be undertaken by all those in the school, including middle leaders, teachers and the community. Most importantly, it also includes the voices of students because it is they who experience the impact of the culture most directly. As an inquiry team leader who led a mathematics inquiry said after she interviewed a group of Year 6 students about what it was like to learn mathematics at her school:

> *Certainly, the student voice is really important, because what the students are telling you is not always what the teachers think. We think we are doing a great job and they say well actually ... yeah. They thought we were slow and boring. We thought we were being nice to them!*
>
> Inquiry Leader, Prep–6 school

The bottom line for leaders is that, if they do not become conscious of the cultures in their school then those cultures will manage them. Understanding organisational culture is important for everyone, but it is essential for leaders to have a particularly deep understanding of culture if they are to lead effectively (Schein, 2017).

Intentionally create a learning culture

Just examining the school culture won't change it. A learning culture needs to be intentionally created, otherwise the default will be the existing, overarching school culture. Once the existing school culture is identified, ask, 'What do we need to do to create the sort of learning culture we want?' 'Do leaders and teachers see themselves as learners and how does this relate to their own students as learners?' Intentionally creating a learning culture means prioritising its development as something the whole school will focus on.

A challenging and vulnerable time for leaders is during the change process. It can be unsettling for established members and can lead to high staff turnover as everyone looks to a more stable past through 'rose-tinted glasses'. That attrition, in turn, leads to a need to induct new members into a culture in transition. Once a strong learning culture is created, however, new arrivals will enter into a set of norms and ways of being that are an expected part of 'how things are done around here'.

Catalysts for change can take various forms. Typically, these involve some kind of challenging event or an urgent need identified through evidence that challenges current thinking and prompts a shared recognition of the need to create a new culture. For example, the explicit realisation that a school is not performing as well as once thought and not all students are achieving to the best of their potential can prompt this need. A new deputy principal, who came to school that was rapidly losing students and staff after years of low achievement and problematic student behaviour, used the spiral of inquiry (see the Introduction) as a mechanism for creating a new culture. She explains how their new culture started:

> *The school was at rock bottom really, but we had a new leadership team. That was a huge catalyst. We had some people that were really inspired to make change. We had our data but that wasn't something that people had really seen with clear eyes before. It was sort of looked at but no one had really analysed it and really understood what it could tell them or what it meant. And I think the third one was the on-boarding of staff. Before the spiral of inquiry really kicked in people weren't talking with each other about learning and teaching or the whole idea of professional learning teams. So, the whole on-boarding of staff, all talking about the same thing, all wanting to be better at the same thing. I think it's sort of three layers there. So, leadership, data and staff coming together to do something.*
>
> Deputy Principal, K–8 school

Leaders have a central role in leading change in organisational culture; however, in the process of changing culture it is important not to throw out what is already working well. Successful organisations simultaneously promote both stability and change, they keep the good things going while working to improve the things that need changing. Some follow-up questions from Box 2.1 are identified in Box 2.2.

BOX 2.2
Culture Change Tool

When you have identified the school culture using the School Culture Tool in the previous section, ask:
- What aspects of the organisational culture currently support a learning culture?
- What is worth keeping and maintaining for stability?
- What is working against creating a learning culture?
- What needs to go or change?
- How will we do this?

Tackle the tough stuff

Leading a learning culture means tackling the tough things. For example, a strong learning culture involves disagreement and disequilibrium as teachers and leaders continually ask questions and debate issues of practice (Fullan & Hargreaves, 1996). It can be tempting, as a leader, to avoid the tough issues, to ignore the negative comments and to proceed as if everyone is 'on board'; however, this is rarely effective. Instead, it is important to uncover people's views and to talk about the issues as a deputy principal working through the change process explains:

> *Absolutely I understood how they felt and I kept saying at every staff meeting, 'We're "in the fog" as we work through this, and it's okay, it's okay to feel like this. We're just playing with it. Nothing's set in stone. It's okay'. That only resonated with some personalities. One staff member was going, 'This is not okay. I don't know what's going on'.*
>
> Deputy Principal, K–6 school

One helpful tool is to focus on 'perspective checking' (see Box 2.3). Different people in the school will have different perspectives and these are all significant in tackling tough issues. Perspective checking involves finding out the different viewpoints and trying to understand the reasons for them. Importantly, perspective checking helps to identify what might be changed to enable a learning culture in which such perspectives can change.

BOX 2.3
Perspective Checking Tool

As a school leadership team, consider a decision you have to make and ask:
- Who are the different people/groups that this decision will affect?
- Check: Have you thought of everyone/every group?
- Next ask yourself, 'If I were to ask them what they think, what do we expect they would say?' This is your 'best guess'.

Next check your 'best guess' with them and ask:
- What do they actually think?
- Were you right?
- What did you learn about their perspective that you were not previously aware of and how will this inform your decision making?

To tackle the tough stuff effectively you need to create safety and support for learning. Safety and support can be provided, for example, by making it clear that disagreement is accepted and is an important way of surfacing important issues. Bypassing disagreement is a common default way of working but, in fact, disagreement does not go away just because you don't talk about it! Safety and support are created by having an expectation that conversations will involve disagreement and this is okay. A learning culture will always be a little uncomfortable, however, because it needs to challenge existing beliefs, support students and improve practice; this often demands questioning the assumptions, beliefs and practices that currently drive decisions about learning and teaching.

Keep the focus on students

A learning culture keeps learning central to 'the way we do things around here'. But it is not just any learning—it is learning that focuses on improving outcomes for students. Effective learning cultures 'backwards map' from student learning needs to teachers' professional learning to leadership learning. A culture that focuses on teacher learning alone in the absence of a focus on students' learning needs will not be effective in making a difference for students or create a learning culture. One way of thinking about how to keep the focus on students is to consider the instructional triangle, a model of the embedded nature of a learning culture, as shown in Figure 2.1.

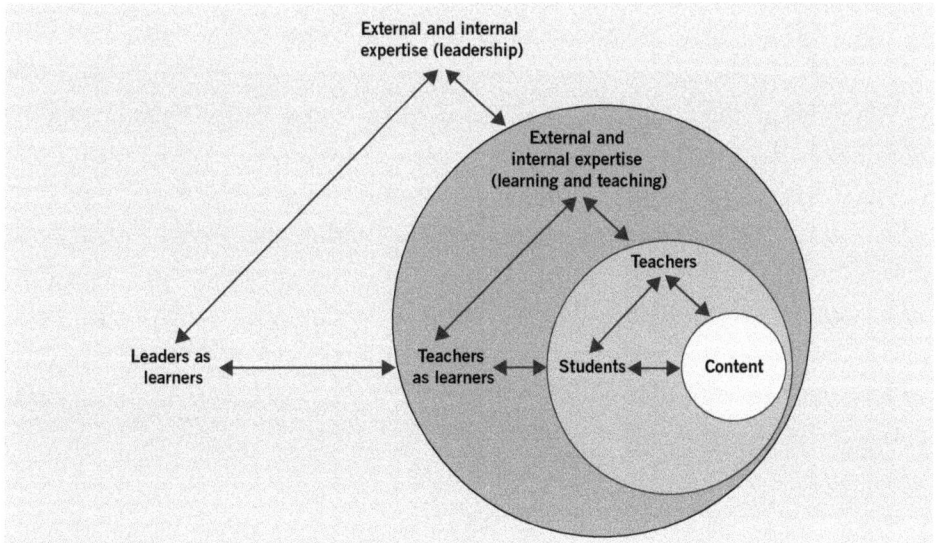

FIGURE 2.1: The embedded nature of a learning culture

In the small circle at the bottom right we can see the content. The content is the focus of learning for the students and may include skills, knowledge and dispositions. The instructional triangle represents how students, teachers and content interact.

Moving the lens out from here to the next circle is the professional learning of teachers. This triangle represents the instructional triangle for teacher learning. Here, the teacher is the learner. Facilitation of their learning at this point is provided by both external expertise (for example, professional developers) and that which is internal to the school (for example, the principal, teacher leaders, professional learning networks). At this level, the content or focus for professional learning becomes the work of classroom teaching—the interaction between teachers, students and content is represented inside the teacher learning circle.

Moving out now to the largest triangle is the whole-school context of school improvement. Within this triangle, the school leader is located as the learner. Again, facilitation of learning is the responsibility of both internal and external expertise to the school. However, the 'content' or 'focus' of professional learning now becomes everything in the larger circle: both the teachers' learning about their practice and the students' learning about content become part of the leaders' learning about how the school works and the development of the learning culture.

Figure 2.1 might serve as a useful tool for of identifying the connection (or lack of) between students' learning needs, teachers' learning focus and school leaders' learning focus. Everyone is involved. In Chapter 1 we described this as 'vertical coherence'.

When trying to change things in a school, it can be tempting to engage in one of the many professional learning programs on offer. A focus on students means that decisions about professional learning for leaders and teachers need to be based on the learning needs of students rather than the availability of particular professional learning programs. The key questions are: 'What do our students need to learn?', 'What are the professional learning needs of our teachers to enable them to support student learning?' and 'What is it that we, as leaders, need to learn to support our teachers to improve outcomes for student learners?'

Engage everyone in genuine inquiry

It has been said that lawyers and teachers are the only professionals who ask questions to which they already know the answers! An important part of a learning culture is engaging people in genuine inquiry, asking questions to which they (and you) do not already know the answer, and which come from a place of curiosity and a genuine desire to know and learn. People tend to use questions to cross-examine each other but, '… these questions are wrong-footed from the start. They emerge from a purpose of trying to persuade the other person that you are right and they are wrong, rather than trying to learn' (Stone, Patton, & Heen, 2010, p. 174).

Working with the spiral of inquiry (see the Introduction) can help in creating and maintaining a learning culture. The spiral of inquiry positions leaders' and teachers' actions in a cycle of intentional and ongoing inquiry about what is going on for learners and how the professionals (including the school culture) may be contributing to the identified issues.

Something to be aware of, however, is that not all inquiry is the same. In fact, much of what is referred to as inquiry is actually inquiry in name only. One of the problems is that asking a question has typically been assumed to mean a genuine need to know, however, this is far from reality. Many questions are asked without the motivation of wanting to learn, which is central to genuine inquiry. Such questions might resemble inquiry on the surface but the motivation is actually manipulative or testing to see if others agree with your solution. Inquiries that begin from these motivations are 'pseudo-inquiries' and need to be identified as such because they take away time and energy from genuine inquiry.

On the other hand, inquiry that is genuine is driven by the desire to learn through a stance of open-mindedness and curiosity. It is marked by open-mindedness, when people are receptive to alternative possibilities and willing to think again despite having formulated a view. Table 2.1 gives some examples that distinguish between genuine inquiry, and manipulative and testing inquiries that are both forms of pseudo-inquiry.

Something you might do is to begin noticing when you ask or hear a question that is not actually intended to elicit a point of view to explore. It can be eye opening to realise just how many times a day this happens. An important suggestion for inquiry: '… if you don't really have a question, then don't ask a question' (Stone et al., 2010, p. 174).

TABLE 2.1: Examples of genuine and pseudo-inquiry

Genuine inquiry questions	Pseudo-inquiry questions	
	Manipulative question	Testing question
We discussed the issue of student motivation and if it would make any difference if we used real-life contexts for mathematics word problems. So, what happened when you tried this?	Are word problems a good way to teach addition when we know that children usually answer them incorrectly?	Which of your students are at Level 4?
We talked about engaging with small group discussion in science. Has anyone tried it? What happened? What have we learned?	Is there time for discussion in science when we have so many competing priorities?	How did your class go in the last science post-test?

Use the spiral of inquiry to develop and sustain a learning culture

The spiral of inquiry (see the Introduction) is helpful in making visible the school culture and achieving the work of developing a learning culture. During the scanning phase, focus intentionally on trying to understand what drives 'the way we do things around here' (the organisational culture). It can then be possible to ask the question, 'Is the way we do things around here working for our students?' (the beginning of a learning culture). A key concern is, 'Will our ways of working achieve equity and meet the needs of our most vulnerable students?'

After exploring current ways of working and student experience, and deciding on a focus, the next step is in 'developing a hunch'. Here leaders and teachers work together to explore how they could be contributing to outcomes for students within the current school culture. You may want to ask the questions in Box 2.4.

BOX 2.4
Questions about school culture when 'developing a hunch'
- How does what we do and what we value influence the way things happen in our school?
- What are the beliefs that are driving our current school culture?
- How has this come about?
- Why does it continue?

These questions are often a challenge to genuine inquiry because they involve questioning the deeper aspects of the organisational culture.

It can be valuable to engage educators and professional learning facilitators from outside the school in this phase. Why? Because, as the saying goes, 'a fish would likely be the last creature to discover water'. When you are immersed in something and it is your everyday existence, it can be difficult to become aware of it. Sometimes it takes stepping outside your familiar context or culture (such as going to another school or having an outsider come in and share what they notice) to help make things visible. It is not until they are visible that you can intentionally work on deciding what parts of the current school culture support a learning culture you want to nurture—and what parts are getting in the way that you want to change.

Once you have some clarity and shared understandings about how the actions of the professionals, and the culture in which they are embedded, impact on student learning, the next phases are learning and taking action. As stated in the introductory chapter, these phases interact with one another. You might ask, 'What do we need to learn and change to develop the learning culture we value?' This can be an uncomfortable stage as the way you used to do things and what you used to value is changing.

Sometimes this sort of change is imposed from outside, but this is never wholly successful. Because school culture is made up of the values, actions and beliefs of the people within the school, these very people need to value and to want to change 'the way we do things around here'. Box 2.5 has some questions you may like to ask yourselves. External expertise can also be valuable for facilitating difficult discussions and pointing out possible inconsistencies or directions, as well as for supporting leaders as they work through this process—but an externally driven or mandated process is unlikely to result in cultural change.

BOX 2.5
Questions for checking changes in school culture
- Are we achieving the sort of learning culture we intended?
- How is this impacting on student learning and wellbeing?
- How can we know?
- What are the experiences of our learners, of our students, of our teachers and of our leaders?

The spiral of inquiry can provide a structure for shifting to a learning culture and provides a shared language for talking about what is happening and why. Making the learning culture itself the subject of inquiry opens up space for addressing difficult issues in a genuine way. A teacher explains her experience like this:

> *When we were challenged on our views about whether or not we would make a difference to the learning of students who came from low-income families that did not have a history of success in schooling, what I think happened is that the racist comments that had been made during meetings in the past just went underground. People still said that stuff they just didn't say it publicly. Interestingly, this actually pretty much stopped after we talked as a staff about what sort of culture we want[ed] in our school.*
>
> Teacher, Yr 9–12 school

Conclusion

The need to establish a learning culture in which to locate professional learning highlights the issue of complexity in change as described in the Introduction. Many previous efforts have treated change and improvement as merely complicated—'We can fix things one bit at a time'. As a result, they have failed. The 'bits' need to be embedded in a much wider whole of 'how we do things and learn around here'.

Leaders have a crucial role in creating and maintaining a strong learning culture, in fact they are the main 'architects of culture' (Schein, 2017). This responsibility demands the asking of and responding to questions such as 'What values and beliefs do we want to have drive the way we do things around here?' and 'What structural changes and resources are necessary to enable this?' A strong learning culture focuses on a few, key student-focused goals and provides a coherent and connected way of working that meets the needs of all learners, including teachers and leaders. While it may seem relatively straightforward to understand the key principles of creating a strong learning culture, actually enacting these is much more difficult. Being clear about what the school is trying to achieve in a learning culture, recognising the inherent challenges and continually problem solving to address these is an ongoing and important part of leading a culture of learning. A school culture that is not aligned with a learning culture will consistently undermine any initiatives. Under these circumstances, changing the existing culture is central to leading professional learning with impact.

CHAPTER 3
Emotion, uncertainty and vulnerability

The challenge
New learning creates inevitable uncertainty, vulnerability and increased emotion for teachers and leaders. Yet emotion is often overlooked in the planning and implementation of professional learning and, more often than not, shows up as an unwelcome and troublesome guest for leaders to deal with. With care and attention, social-emotional aspects of the professional and student learning environments can be enhanced, resulting in better outcomes for all.

It is an ongoing frustration for leaders that some teachers do not appear to engage with professional learning or make proposed changes to their practice. Their apparent refusal to engage and rejection of new ideas are often interpreted as resistance to change. It is easy to assume that these teachers do not want to make the changes—or have not put in the necessary time and effort to learn the knowledge and skills needed to do so. However, this is frequently inaccurate, and our research shows that 'teacher resistance' is not a useful way to try to explain a lack of change or the way to address it (Twyford et al., 2017).

In our interviews with teachers, we have found that many teachers feel vulnerable and respond emotionally to the uncertainty surrounding their new learning and the expectations of change. They perceive engagement as coming with high levels of risk to themselves, both professionally and personally. Even their identity as a teacher can feel undermined.

The challenge for leaders is to understand and identify the sources of uncertainty in professional learning that cause teachers to experience these emotions. It then becomes possible to reduce unnecessary uncertainty and minimise overall perceived risk, thus increasing teacher engagement with change. Reducing uncertainty and perceptions of risk is harder when professional learning involves surfacing and challenging problematic beliefs and biases such as addressing inequity in outcomes for students (see Chapter 5). The sensitive, and sometimes political, nature of this work can heighten feelings of vulnerability and increase perceptions of risk that, if ignored, can derail improvement efforts.

What leaders do matters. Leaders can inadvertently increase or decrease teachers' perceptions of risk through their interactions and the learning culture they create (Twyford & Le Fevre, 2019). It is important to realise, however, that leaders also experience emotion, vulnerability and perceived risk when leading this improvement work, especially when confronted with teachers who do not appear to be engaged, as this principal identified:

> *Professional learning and teachers' perceptions of risk. I think it's really important to acknowledge it and to think and have that in your planning and that how we approach them as leaders, middle leaders, whatever you are, that we need to be aware of it because it has impact. And the way that we approach things, the way that we plan things can either be positive or negative in terms of the way we get teachers to implement it. So, it's worthwhile having foresight and thinking about it before you launch into something… So, if I was to do something, I'd want to get people's perception on it, 'What are you thinking?'*
>
> Principal, K–6 school

The reason why this is a challenge

Teaching is full of uncertainty as described in the now well-recognised quote as 'the wildly uncertain triangle defined by the teacher's own ambivalent self, that bunch of unpredictable kids and the always slippery subject' (McDonald, 1992, p. 13). Now, if anything, uncertainty has increased with the development of sophisticated communication information technologies, the rapid progress in knowledge, and the drive by educational policy in some countries to encourage schools to engage in multiple professional learning and change initiatives concurrently. Nothing seems good enough anymore, with constant questions being asked about the meaning of progress, the ways to achieve it and the difficulties of knowing what has been achieved. Of course, uncertainty increases when change is expected, thus heightening the likelihood of an emotional response.

Many leaders can recount stories of high levels of emotion related to change. It is usually believed to be an inevitable yet problematic accompaniment to change, with some privately thinking, 'better left at the school gate'. Why are we uncomfortable talking about emotion?

> *Oh, I think there's a level of anxiety, I hear this from heaps of principals and leaders in schools, that there's always that anxiety and risk particularly around being watched and being ... having observations in our professional learning. It doesn't matter how long you've been doing it, it still tends to pop up, and I know that they do. So, I do talk about this.*
>
> *Principal, K–6 school*

Historically, emotion, cognition, and motivation were considered separate and oppositional processes, with emotion seen as a weakness and troublesome. Now it is clear that they, in fact, work together in complex, inseparable ways, with emotion now seen to be a critical gatekeeper of learning (Dumont et al., 2010). There is, however, an ongoing legacy from these earlier beliefs about emotion. Although this is changing, researchers and policymakers have been wary of studying or addressing emotion and have tended to focus on the structural and operational elements of improvement initiatives rather than the emotional aspects. Emotion, particularly expressions of anxiety or vulnerability, is just an undesirable side effect.

In reality, emotion is everywhere. Everyone, knowingly or unknowingly, brings a dynamic 'emotional state' to everything they do. Engagement in professional learning and school improvement often heighten emotions and increase perceptions of risk through the new uncertainties created. Risk in this context is not about danger—it is all about uncertainty. What is expected of me? Will I have to change? Will I be able to? Do I want to? The private answers to these questions impact on teachers' actions, which, in turn, shape the reactions of others. These thoughts recycle to inform future perceptions of risk, particularly if their experience has been negative (Twyford et al., 2017).

Emotion associated with risk can be expressed as feelings of vulnerability. Teachers describe vulnerability as inward looking, occurring when there is a possibility of feeling embarrassed, losing confidence, failing themselves and their students, or a more intense feeling that their personal and professional identities and efficacy are challenged (Twyford et al., 2017). Feelings of vulnerability increase with exposure to others. Classroom observations and working collaboratively are particular contexts where vulnerability can increase.

> *I think they just don't like the whole idea of being observed. I don't know if it's a personal thing or just self-esteem issues; I've never heard so many issues about observations. Like [for] some teachers it's almost an anxiety*

> *attack. It's like, 'Are you serious? It's just an ob'. And the video thing. Maybe it just comes down to the individual teachers. Some teachers go for it, see it as an opportunity to learn from what has been observed and maybe some teachers see it as they don't want you to see what they do. And then there's some that are just not confident.*
>
> *School Leader, K–6 school*

Uncertainty in professional learning can be considered across three broad, sequential categories: existing uncertainty as a result of previous experiences; uncertainty in anticipation of future events, such as an imminent observation of practice; and uncertainty about the possible consequences of that future event (see Figure 3.1). Within each category, uncertainty arises from a variety of different sources. Collectively, this uncertainty frames how teachers (and leaders) make sense of what is going on for them in their changing environment.

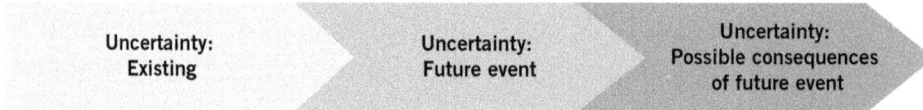

FIGURE 3.1: Categories of uncertainty

Individuals make their own sense of uncertainty. This sense, in turn, influences their levels of perceived risk and vulnerability. Some individuals will perceive more risk than others. Teachers who experience high perceived risk report strong emotional responses and negative learning experiences. Typically, these teachers seek reassurance to build confidence, ask for help predominantly from trusted others, are likely to over-prepare for an event and deliver lessons that are less 'risky' when they are being observed. On the other hand, teachers who perceive no, or minimal, risk take actions that are more likely to enhance their learning, such as invite others to observe them and provide feedback, and ask for help from those likely to build their knowledge and challenge them.

Relationships and knowledge are two key factors that differentiate those likely to feel highly vulnerable and those who are less so. Teachers readily take risks when they feel secure in both their relationships with others with whom they work and are confident in their knowledge of the content of the professional learning and how to enact new practices. If one of these factors is lower, teachers may still be prepared to take risks and try new things. For example, trusting relationships encourage those with gaps in their knowledge to be vulnerable and take risks to fill in those gaps. Similarly, having knowledge provides confidence to take risks when relationships are less secure. However, teachers are less likely to take risks in their learning, and may even avoid situations where their practice is visible, when they are not confident about their knowledge and uncertain about their relationships with those promoting learning and change. This teacher expressed it like this:

> *I think there's so many changes and there's so many things you have to do, that sometimes it just becomes, 'Oh gosh, that's another thing'. And so, you can be not on board at the beginning. But I think once you gain that knowledge and you're comfortable and you feel okay about it and the people you are working with, then the risk decreases.*
>
> Teacher, K–6 school

Most of us familiar with the concept of resistance probably react unconsciously to teachers' actions from a 'resistance frame'. However, it can be helpful to deliberately consider uncertainty and vulnerability as alternative explanations for lack of change or engagement. Thinking about uncertainty shifts the focus from the teacher to include the professional learning environment and leaders as co-learners in this environment. This opens the possibility for leaders to take different actions to address the challenge of emotion in the process of change.

Leadership actions to address the challenge

All the suggested actions that follow involve talking about emotion, uncertainty, risk and vulnerability in some form or another. This can be particularly challenging for action-oriented leaders who like to get things done and may overlook the social-emotional aspect of being a learner. Yet if teachers feel vulnerable, uncertain and anxious it is difficult for them to learn. Successful learning and change involve experimenting with new practices, having some failures and trying again. It is not possible to eliminate uncertainty, nor is it desirable, because of the complex nature of teaching and how to make it more effective. It is possible, however, to reduce unnecessary uncertainty, to make visible the different sources of uncertainty and work with teachers to live with those uncertainties that cannot be changed.

We have provided several tools to help leaders to scaffold their own learning and feel more comfortable about talking about risk and emotion in the learning and change process, and thus be more successful in having all teachers engage in improvement activities.

Help others understand the role of emotion in professional learning

Engaging in professional learning is an emotional experience. Very often, when planning professional learning initiatives, the focus is on what and how teachers will learn. For example, leaders often ask: 'What should the focus of teacher learning be?' 'How will we engage teachers in professional learning in ways that enable them to learn and change their practice?' Less often asked are questions such as 'How might teachers feel about being asked to change their practice?', 'What effect might new learning have on a teacher's sense of themselves as professionals?' or, 'What might a teacher perceive as a risk when being asked to share evidence of their practice with others?'

Recognising the role of emotion in the change process for teachers and leaders is key to figuring out ways to reduce negative emotion and provide appropriate support. It is not enough to know what and how one is going to learn. It is also essential to understand how a learner will feel and experience their learning. As one principal shared with a school leader:

> *Sometimes you approach people like a tornado, and it's right in your face and you actually need to be a gentle sea breeze sometimes, because actually people respond to that—they look like you're going to blow them off the earth.*
>
> *Principal, K–6 school*

Failing to explicitly address the emotional aspects of learning often results in people avoiding new change initiatives. Both understanding the role of emotion in professional learning yourself, as a leader, and using this knowledge to help others understand it, are points at which leaders can potentially reduce teachers' perceptions of risk and their feelings of vulnerability. Talking about change and what is involved in professional learning is a powerful way to help people understand what to expect and reduce uncertainty. Making public what you experience as a leader acknowledges that emotion is an inevitable part of learning and change and is sometimes uncomfortable or even distressing. Providing teachers with structured opportunities to do the same can open up conversations and potentially identify commonalities between the concerns of leaders and those of teachers. The tool in Box 3.1 can provide this kind of structure early in the change process and be used to review progress at future points in time.

BOX 3.1
Creating a visual representation of emotions about change

Co-construct a visual representation of how people are feeling about a proposed change. Leaders and teachers have different coloured post-it notes and write down how they are feeling. Provide possible headings such as:
- feeling sure/unsure
- feeling excited/not excited
- feeling confident/unconfident
- think/don't think it will be worth the effort.

Place these on a whiteboard with leaders' notes on one side and teachers' notes on the other. When anyone from either group identifies the same emotion, place these in the middle. Discuss the 'group only' responses and the overlaps and work out together what the implications are for moving forward.

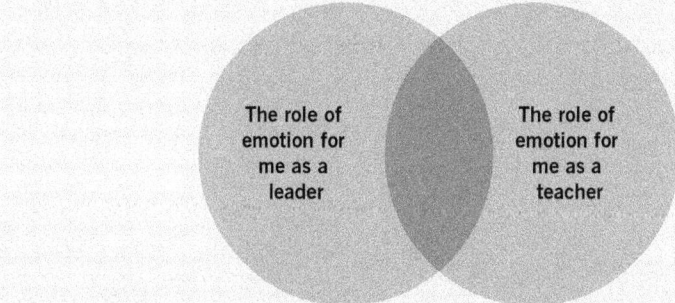

Understand, notice and reduce unnecessary uncertainty

There will always be uncertainty as part of learning and change but not all uncertainty is useful or necessary. So where is uncertainty likely to occur? What does it look like? How do we as leaders contribute to it? Can we deliberately reduce it? The first thing to know is what the sources of uncertainty might be. As identified in Figure 3.1, categories of uncertainty can be grouped according to those existing, those anticipated and the possible consequences of future events.

Existing uncertainty involves those misgivings that teachers and leaders already have. They may come from prior experiences of professional learning, with negative experiences more likely to be recalled than positive ones. Individuals respond to existing in-school processes, such as appraisal and employment status, and how these have been impacted by engagement in professional learning on previous occasions.

Uncertainty connected to future professional learning events generally connects to one or more of the following: relationships, knowledge, purpose, organisation and evidence. Relationships can be a core source of uncertainty. Teachers may feel uncertain whether their relationships in the professional learning environment will be sufficiently supportive to encourage their risk taking. This involves notions of trust, support, respect and being known as a learner.

> *If you don't have the relationship with the people—we are like the kids. If you don't have that relationship, you're not prepared to take the risk.*
>
> Teacher, K–6 school

Uncertainty around knowing the 'what' and 'how' of professional learning is common. As learners, teachers wonder about the adequacy of their knowledge and skills relative to their perception of what will be expected. They can have concerns about putting things into practice or feel confused about expectations. These concerns can happen at any stage of new learning and change.

Lack of clarity or uncertainty connected to the purpose and organisational details can create doubts over the reason for professional learning and whether it will be positive for their students. Not having enough detail and certainty around the organisational processes, such as scheduling for observations, also adds to uncertainty. This principal found ways to mitigate this feeling:

> *For me it was the organisation that's really important. We need to make sure that the schedule's out and then the release is so people have got plenty of time to soak it in and absorb it and they're ready—rather than just hand it in the week before and everyone's running around like headless chooks.*
>
> Principal, K–6 school

The use of evidence about 'performance' also creates uncertainty. Teachers wonder how evidence, such as videos of practice or observation notes and discussion minutes, will be used for non-professional learning purposes, such as appraisal and employment-related decisions.

The final broad category of uncertainty arises from anticipation of possible consequences of the future professional learning event(s). Some teachers worry about the impact of professional learning on their workloads, how 'successful' they will be and, most importantly, whether their students' learning will improve as a result of their engagement, as these two teachers expressed:

> *I suppose the biggest perception is that maybe it won't work and then it's wasting your time. That it's not right for your students. That you don't think it's particularly applicable.*
>
> Teacher, K–6 school

> *But I think anything new ... You can be open for it and take it but there's still always a little bit of risk maybe, where you've got to maybe introduce it into your class, it's something you don't know whether [or not] it's going to work. So, I think there's always an element of risk. It might not be super high or anything, but there is an element of risk.*
>
> Teacher, Yr 7–12 school

Collectively, these sources of uncertainty provide a map for leaders to use when proposing new professional learning as part of their schooling improvement work. The audit tool in Box 3.2 can raise awareness and help to pinpoint possible current sources of uncertainty, identify areas for further analysis, and inform the actions that could be taken to remove or mitigate uncertainty and vulnerability. Some possible examples are provided.

BOX 3.2
Uncertainty Audit Tool

Consider what evidence you have in relation to the different sources of uncertainty in the current situation and discuss with teachers. Identify what further evidence you may need for the areas needing further analysis and the possible actions to remove or mitigate risk. Decide on how and when you will monitor and review progress in relation to the different categories.

Category	Source of uncertainty in each category	Describe the current situation	Identify areas for further analysis	Possible actions to remove/ mitigate	Monitor and review
Existing uncertainty	**Prior professional learning** What experiences have teachers had in professional learning?	Last year's PL was unsuccessful for students, lots of energy wasted		Listen to teacher voice about their concerns	
	Individual responses	Some teachers visibly upset		Know teachers as learners	
	Existing school practices What existing systems and practices increase uncertainty?	Appraisal is done by the professional learning observer		Remove or mitigate unnecessary uncertainty	

BOX 3.2 (continued)

Category	Source of uncertainty in each category	Describe the current situation	Identify areas for further analysis	Possible actions to remove/mitigate	Monitor and review
Uncertainty: Future event	**Relationships** Do I know this person well enough to …?	External facilitator not known by many staff	Analyse for potential conflicts	• Consider the group dynamics • Build relationships	
	Knowledge, what and how Do I have the knowledge and skills to do what's expected?	• Some teachers never used inquiry • New learning gaps larger for some	Find out levels of knowledge and confidence	Provide additional support for first-timers	Proactively check on how people are feeling
	Organisation and purpose of the PL Do I know enough about ….?	• Teachers don't know why • Schedules not clear and change	• Are inquiries focused on proving or improvement? • Is 'failure' OK?		
	Use of evidence • What will be used to judge me and my practice? • How will this be used?	Inquiry is part of appraisal	• Are inquiries focused on proving or improvement? • Is 'failure' OK?		

Uncertainty: Possible consequences	**Consequences for self**
	• Teachers
	• Leaders
	  –What time and effort?
	  –Will I get it right?
		Workload	Audit additional meeting time	Listen to teacher talk— failure or improvement	

	Consequences for others • Students • Family	• Concerns about additional class time • Who is observation data shared with?	Conduct student and parent voice evidence		

BOX 3.3
Survey of perceived risk and willingness

At a staff meeting, ask teachers to fill in this survey anonymously. If it is done electronically, a summary of the results can be put up immediately with the implications discussed by everyone involved. If completed on paper, or you want to give yourself a bit more time, then present the results at the next staff meeting and ask teachers for their interpretations and the implications.

Directions
For each statement, rate by **CIRCLING ONE** number.
1. The extent to which you are willing to do this on a scale from 1 to 6.
2. The extent to which you perceive doing this as a risk on a scale from 1 to 6.

Statement	Extent to which I am willing to do this						Extent to which I perceive this as a risk					
	Not willing				Very willing		No risk				High risk	
1. Analysing and interpreting my student outcomes with colleagues and school leaders	1	2	3	4	5	6	1	2	3	4	5	6
2. Participating in spirals of inquiry with colleagues I don't know	1	2	3	4	5	6	1	2	3	4	5	6
3. Sharing my beliefs and hunches with colleagues as part of spirals of inquiry	1	2	3	4	5	6	1	2	3	4	5	6
4. Sharing my beliefs and hunches with school leaders as part of spirals of inquiry	1	2	3	4	5	6	1	2	3	4	5	6
5. Challenging the views of my colleagues in front of others when our views differ	1	2	3	4	5	6	1	2	3	4	5	6
6. Challenging the views of my school leaders in front of others when our views differ	1	2	3	4	5	6	1	2	3	4	5	6
7. Trying new teaching practices without certainty that current outcomes will improve	1	2	3	4	5	6	1	2	3	4	5	6
8. Teaching in front of my colleagues as I begin to implement expected changes in my practice	1	2	3	4	5	6	1	2	3	4	5	6
9. Teaching in front of my school leaders as I begin to implement expected changes in my practice	1	2	3	4	5	6	1	2	3	4	5	6
10. Teaching in front of colleagues once I feel more competent with the expected changes in my practice	1	2	3	4	5	6	1	2	3	4	5	6
11. Teaching in front of my school leaders once I feel more competent with the expected changes	1	2	3	4	5	6	1	2	3	4	5	6
12. *Add your own*	1	2	3	4	5	6	1	2	3	4	5	6

Sometimes it can be helpful to find out what particular events or activities within a professional learning initiative are perceived as risks. Things leaders anticipate will be problematic may not be—and vice versa! One way of finding out teachers' perceptions is to survey them. The survey in Box 3.3 is designed to find out about teachers' perceptions about different parts of a professional learning initiative and to identify where teachers need particular support, experience vulnerability and require assurances of trusting relationships. You may want to use the results when completing the audit tool in Box 3.2. This, or any other survey, can be tailored to the features of professional learning that are relevant in your context.

To understand, notice and reduce uncertainty, sometimes it is sufficient to just complete a survey like this, as it provides a common text from which people can talk about their experiences, share their views and discuss what sorts of support they feel would enable them to take the next step in their development as teachers. At other times, further steps, such as facilitated discussion or explicit provision of tailored support, might be needed to address concerns and reduce uncertainty.

Consider risk, not resistance

It is common to hear leaders talking about teachers as 'resisting' change or being resistant to a new idea. There is a tendency to make assumptions about the motivations and reasons behind others' actions, particularly when they appear to be disengaged or even antagonistic about a professional learning or change initiative. For example, a teacher may perceive that they will not be regarded by others as being effective if they have to change what they are doing. They may fear failure or feel that they do not have the necessary knowledge and skills to do something differently. The 'safe' thing to do is to keep doing what they already know how to do. This might inaccurately be viewed as being resistant, when in fact what is going on is the teacher is feeling highly vulnerable, which interferes with their capacity to engage fully with the change. Listen for the language of resistance identified in the wordle in Figure 3.2 when teachers engage in or discuss the worth of professional learning activities and expected change.

A potentially powerful leadership action is to consider the possibility that perceptions of risk and vulnerabilities might be at play and check your assumptions about why people may not be engaging. There is a double bind when considering risk. Everyone needs to take risks to learn and change, yet too much risk decreases the willingness to try. When the balance tips towards perceiving too much risk in a change process, learning (and sometimes participation) is likely to stop.

As perceptions of risk and feelings of vulnerability decrease, listen for the positive talk of change and the words in the wordle in Figure 3.3 emerge.

An advantage of framing such actions as risk rather than resistance is that it shifts the focus from the teacher being 'the problem' to thinking about learning and change as risk-taking, so trying to understand what is happening for the teachers in the face of these risks. This means recognising when emotions associated with change might be a distraction and seeking to understand and act in ways to mitigate them in order to progress the learning and change agenda. This shift in focus also shifts responsibility from the teacher having the primary responsibility for change, to leaders and teachers working together to

FIGURE 3.2: Wordle of resistance language

FIGURE 3.3: Wordle of risk language

make it as emotionally safe as possible for everyone to engage in the learning and change agenda.

Support others to take risks

Emotion, uncertainty and vulnerability are experienced differently by different people. Teachers engaging in the same professional learning initiative, for example, can have vastly different emotional reactions, with one teacher feeling excited while another might feel highly anxious. The problem is that the teacher who feels highly anxious might disguise this by acting as if overconfident, not asking for help or behaving as if they don't care. This is in part because, in society, being open about one's emotional reactions is not encouraged—we are encouraged to appear invulnerable.

> *I think that climate of supporting—you know, not being judgemental on what you're doing. Yeah, you've got to accept that people will stuff up if you want them to take risks. That's what risks are about isn't it? It's that supportive—whether it's implied or explicit, it doesn't really matter. You soon learn. You can be safe ... There still are times when you become defensive. Making mistakes, it's not very comfortable but it's not—yeah it's part of the risk management too. As I said, it sent me back to, 'Let me make mistakes, don't punish me for them. Don't bring them up again; just let me make them. But yeah, if I'm making the same one time and time [again], maybe then you could give me a little nudge, but just let me learn'.*
>
> School Leader, Yr 7–12 school

It is important that you, as a leader, know your teachers as 'learners', just as you expect them to know their students as learners. In doing so, you can understand their reactions and work with them to figure out ways to engage and support them to take risks and develop a mindset that taking risks is a part of learning. Interestingly, young people are encouraged to take risks, and yet as adults, we often want to play it safe. The difficulty in judging just how to balance challenge and risk is summed up by this deputy principal:

> *It's the balance, it isn't about making them [the participants] happy. I'm not fooled into thinking I want people to come to me and say, 'Oh, that was so good, I learned so many things to do and I just really like it'. It's not about making them happy or feel good. It's about learning. I don't*

> *know enough, I just go by gut about balance. It's like I walk this rope, I'm not going to shove them to the edge, but I have to find that edge; that's different for individuals, for groups. So, I'm pushing towards it, pushing towards the edge, which is enough disequilibrium to make them have to think, rethink, begin to wonder about stuff, but not enough to have them fall. And I'm ready to catch them if I have pushed too hard.*
> Deputy Principal, Yr 8–12 school

This leader spoke of encouraging teachers to take risks ... but not so many that they would 'fall off the edge'. Those leading the learning and change process need to work with teachers (and leaders) to understand and process their emotions and feelings of vulnerability. This notion of needing to feel secure in order to struggle in front of others is an important one.

One way of thinking about this is to unpack each person's 'learning zone' and where they can take the next step with support. This idea of the learning zone builds on the well-known theoretical notion of the 'zone of proximal development' introduced by Vygotsky (1978). Creating and maintaining the 'learning zone' means finding the place for each individual teacher where they are challenged beyond their comfort zone to learn and take risks, but not pushed to a place where they feel unsafe and are no longer learning.

What is important here is the provision of opportunities to learn and change accompanied by the necessary level of trust and support to function in the learning zone. Teachers in a primary school observed the parallels between how teachers expect students to have safe spaces to try and fail, and to try again and the professional learning spaces in which they were expected to do the same. Two teachers from a K–6 school reflected:

> *I feel that it is necessary to take risk in order to learn in terms of moving outside our comfort zones, just as we encourage children to.*

> *We ask children to take risks with their learning but provide them with the tools and support ... [that] will enable them to achieve success. The same should be true for teachers' professional development.*

Making these parallels explicit for teachers may help them to construct learning environments for themselves that allow them to take deliberate action to make professional learning a safe space for, and to experiment with, change while reducing uncertainty and perceptions of risk.

Understand how trust works

Leaders influence the outcomes of professional learning through their participation. Leaders who do so are more likely to positively influence learner outcomes (Robinson, Lloyd, & Hohepa, 2009). Leaders also influence outcomes through the school cultures they create and their interactions with others (see Chapter 2). They do this through their day-to-day encounters and building trusting relationships. These relationships support risk taking and reduce feelings of vulnerability.

Trust is something that leaders can achieve through interpersonal respect, personal regard for others, competence in their role and personal integrity. Trust can be elusive and knowing about an individual teacher's 'learning zone', their tolerance of uncertainty and the level of trust inherent in different professional learning tasks will help build trust. Above all, a sense of collective trust is needed, where there is 'a sense of confidence that the team will not embarrass, reject, or punish someone for speaking up' (Edmondson, 1999, p. 354).

Trust is not an all or nothing concept but one that is dynamic and highly sensitive to ongoing interactions and responses. High trust at one time does not mean trust still exists at another. As most leaders have experienced, it is easy to lose and difficult to regain.

> *Now I understand it better—when you're trying to change, it's risky, and they need to have that trust. And like that thing that I was talking about—he trusted me to come into his room ... he let me in, and then I helped him and all that sort of stuff and then I stuffed it up. So now it's become a risk for him to ask for help from me, so talking to me he would probably think, 'No, you'll cc people'.*
>
> School Leader, K–6 school

Leaders who engage with teachers as learners, take risks in their learning and become willingly vulnerable to get things wrong are more likely to both develop and maintain the trust of their teachers.

Trust and vulnerability have a paradoxical relationship. Trust is required to be willingly vulnerable, yet vulnerability, especially demonstrated by a leader, leads to greater trust. Trust grows through doing tasks together, but at the same time being mindful of the level of trust required to engage in a shared, but uncertain, learning activity.

Expect and navigate emotion when using the spiral of inquiry

Clarity of purpose about any change reduces uncertainty. What is left unsaid is filled by often inaccurate assumptions. This idea is central to engagement with any change process, regardless of whether an inquiry or other approach is adopted. The more uncertain the process, the greater the importance about establishing a clear purpose at the outset. Many teachers will be asking, 'Why are we doing this inquiry?' 'Isn't my teaching good enough?'

> *I think one of the risks is the evidence might show you're doing a lousy job. You look at it and you think it's not working and therefore you've got to face reality. It's easy for me to keep the Year 10s quiet. They were quiet the other day. They weren't actually learning. You actually can hide those things for a long time but you can't when the evidence is there staring you in the face. Sometimes it confronts you and you have to deal with it ... I can't really put it into words. It's a feeling of you want to know but you don't ... And you rationalise. The idea used to be, oh well that's because they were this and they were that, but really now you need to rationalise what could I have done different or what could have been done? There still are times when you become defensive.*
>
> School Leader, Yr 7–12 school

Issues of uncertainty need also to be addressed throughout the process of inquiry because the focus is usually on complex problems of practice, where ideal solutions are not readily available. The process of searching for novel solutions inevitably creates uncertainty. This issue creates a dilemma for leaders. Prior to engagement in an inquiry process, it is difficult to describe exactly what is expected because it is not a prescriptive process. However, as teachers become more familiar with the process and the changes expected, their perceptions of risk decrease as this classroom teacher described in relation to his new practice being observed:

> *I was most likely to take a risk when it was clear what they wanted me to try. When it was unclear about what I was actually trying to do with my teaching I felt completely flummoxed about what to do. But when it was really clear what they were coming in to look for, it was really helpful when I had seen a model of it or when it wasn't just you know some sort of reading I had to do on a page, when it was really clear about how*

> *it would look, what sort of questions I might ask the kids ... then I was more willing to take those risks because I felt I had a structure. And the goal posts were obvious. Whereas when it's a vague idea, it takes a lot of processing I suppose.*
>
> Classroom Teacher, F–6 school

Another source of uncertainty in any inquiry process is that collaboration is at the centre. Collaboration brings interpersonal uncertainty and the need for trust and safety as explained above. True collaboration also brings diversity of views to the surface where colleagues disagree, which can, in turn, create uncertainty as these views are debated for their worth with the use of evidence.

When it becomes apparent that uncertainty and feelings of vulnerability are inhibiting learning, it may be time to bring out the Uncertainty Audit Tool (Box 3.2), described previously in this chapter, to help pinpoint and address issues that may be inhibiting engagement. If you, as a leader, also engage in the process with teachers, it is more likely to create a shared understanding of the purpose and process for ongoing change.

Conclusion

Emotion, uncertainty and vulnerability are not words commonly seen in books about leading professional learning. Indeed, these important concepts are also uncommon in day-to-day conversations about how to support teacher learning. But they are definitely overheard in the staffroom. It is time that this changed. The role of emotion is central to professional learning and educational change and this is unavoidable. Fortunately, you have influence as a leader and can make a difference by recognising and acknowledging the role of emotion in teacher learning, and indeed in your own work as a leader. It is not enough to just acknowledge it; however, having acknowledged it, take action to reduce perceptions of risk, decrease uncertainty and make vulnerability an acceptable, positive and important aspect of engaging in change.

CHAPTER 4
Evidence and evaluative thinking

The challenge

Genuine and disciplined inquiry is based on the use of evidence. But what evidence? How and why should it be used? When, and by whom? The idea of evidence has, in many settings, come to mean 'hard' or 'objective' evidence only—in particular, the results of standardised or normed assessments. Formal test results are often seen as the only evidence schools have—and they can be dismissed by the often-quoted claims that they do not measure what is valued in the school, they are only a snapshot of one performance by the students and the test format itself reduces the students' ability to respond. As a result, evidence gets a bad name, and the vision of poring over figures and graphs drawing perhaps unwarranted conclusions leads school leaders and their staff to avoid working with evidence and skip straight to what they 'know' from their day-to-day experience of their students and their school.

Schools are awash with many different kinds of evidence that mostly goes unnoticed and unused. It may be numerical (e.g. 'How many students skip which classes?') or it may be more qualitative (e.g. 'Why do they skip more of this class than another?'). Leaders, teachers and students have many rich observations about things that matter but these are rarely systematically collated, discussed or used.

When thinking about the place of evidence in leading and teaching, it is best paired with the idea of evaluative thinking. This thinking is an orientation to inquiry or solving problems of practice that uses evidence to interrupt usual judgement-making processes (Earl & Timperley, 2015). Evidence forms the basis of evaluative thinking and, together, they raise linked challenges for school leaders. Part of the challenge relates to evidence: recognising it, collecting it, interpreting it and understanding its limitations. The other part relates to evaluative thinking. In evaluative thinking, claims and decisions are backed up with evidence and practitioners are constantly seeking evidence of impact. To practise evaluative thinking, school leaders and staff need to know how to use evidence to make improvements and impact student outcomes, suspend judgement and make fewer assumptions when using evidence, use evidence to advance a line of reasoning and use evidence to check if that reasoning was correct. These tasks all require particular skills and mindsets.

The reason why this is a challenge

Establishing a culture of working from, and with, evidence in inquiry and decision making is a challenge for school leaders (Earl & Katz, 2010). It takes practice to slow down, rather than jumping to assumptions based on experience (Katz & Dack, 2013). Particularly in education, where everyone involved must make rapid decisions to 'read' students and is constantly working with emotions and sensitivities (as described in Chapter 3), changing habits of mind to work from evidence rather than 'gut feeling' can be difficult. It is also difficult because the job demands quick judgements and actions, so everyone is practised at making up their minds fast. While this is appropriate in some settings, decision making of this sort often contains unquestioned assumptions and, potentially, unrecognised biases, which will work against the kinds of improvements intended. Slowing down thinking, questioning assumptions and working from evidence takes both discipline and an awareness that require practice.

A further reason why using evidence and evaluative thinking is difficult is that these ways of working permeate the whole inquiry process in all its complexity, so there is not one thing to learn or know, rather there are many skills and understandings that need to be developed. This means that, as leaders and teachers begin to work from an evaluative mindset, there are going to be a series of learning challenges for them to face. Some may involve bringing in outside expertise (for example, learning to interpret sets of evidence) while others may involve connecting staff within the school (for example, teachers of young learners helping teachers of older learners with assessments of reading difficulties).

School leaders and teachers need to understand what can be used as evidence, know how to interpret the evidence, know how to use the evidence to improve outcomes for learners, know what progress would look like in ways that can be checked using evidence and remember to use evidence to evaluate it. For example, in a school that is concerned about problem solving in mathematics, teachers and leaders need to work out what would comprise good evidence of students' problem solving and what aspects of problem solving they want to collect evidence about. Then they need to know how to analyse the evidence, find patterns in it and understand what it is telling them about their students' problem solving. It is easy to collect a lot of solutions to a mathematics word problem, written on paper by students, but will this writing provide the evidence needed? And how can writing from several classes of children be meaningfully combined?

Next, leaders and teachers need to know how they can use what they have found to improve outcomes for learners. How does the evidence tell them what needs to happen next? Finally, they need to work out how they will know if the students are getting better at problem solving. What would the students do if they were better? How could their progress be recorded or described?

Establishing the use of evidence and evaluative thinking in a school requires an understanding that it will not be an overnight change—just providing evidence will not make evaluative thinking happen. Schools that are struggling to embed evaluative thinking in the way they work may have challenges with the type and quality of evidence they have, or with their ability to interpret it. They may then have challenges with putting the evidence to use in making decisions, taking action and checking if they have made a difference. Every school has plenty of evidence but, without an evaluative mindset, it is unlikely to be used to improve outcomes for learners.

Leadership actions to address the challenge

This section provides six leadership actions that can address the challenge of using evidence and developing evaluative thinking in all kinds of education settings. In the first section there is an Evidence Audit Tool that might be a good place to start, no matter where you are on the schooling improvement journey.

Get the evidence in order

Two school leaders were asked to reflect on their schools' use of the spiral of inquiry (see the Introduction) as a framework for professional learning and to improve outcomes for their learners. Asked what the most significant factor was in getting them started on their journey, their first response was 'getting your evidence in order', which they each referred to as 'data':

> *I think the collation of some of our data and the revelation that it had gaps in it was valuable.*
>
> *Deputy Principal, K–6 school*

> *Opening up our data was number one for us. But we had to organise it to make sense of it before we could do that. It wasn't something that people had seen with clear eyes before, so it was sort of looked at but no-one had really analysed it and really understood what it could tell them or what it meant.*
>
> Principal, K–8 school

There is often a lot of evidence that could be used to make decisions and evaluate progress in schools—but equally often it is hard to find, hard to collate and hard to read. There may be more information about some things than others or more of one type of information than other types. Having to do compulsory tests or surveys can make teachers feel that they have done what they need to do by getting learners to complete tasks—and they have no interest in what comes back, or even where the information goes.

Evidence needs to be usable and useful. Usable evidence is accessible (not locked away physically or digitally), in a readable form (not banks of numbers or responses that are hard to read), clean (has unnecessary information removed, has missing information identified, has the information matched to the right learner) and ethically stored and distributed. Useful evidence provides information about valued outcomes and aligns with the questions and concerns of the school.

Two tools follow, in Boxes 4.1 and 4.2, to help you get your evidence in order. They each do different things; either or both of them might apply to your situation, or you might be able to use them as a starting point for devising your own tool or task to help you organise, understand and use your evidence.

The audit tool in Box 4.1 is a way to take stock of what evidence you have available in your school and what state it is in. This would be a useful first task—best tackled by a team of people, be it a senior leadership team, whole staff or a group of staff.

The first tool looks at types of evidence that you might have collected in your school. The second tool, in Box 4.2, is more evaluative and encourages thinking about the adequacy of the evidence you care about. In the first part of the box is a list of the kinds of things you might want evidence about. What is important to you in your professional learning and school improvement work and do you have evidence of a good starting point for your thinking and diagnosis process? This is intended as a list of possible prompts, not as a list of 'should haves', because it depends on your context. For example, you might choose student engagement from the list, then go to the questions at the end to help think about the adequacy of your evidence on student engagement. 'What do we have that would be evidence of student engagement?' 'Is that evidence usable and useful?' and so on.

BOX 4.1
Evidence Audit Tool

Think about each of these types of evidence and what their status is in your school.

In each column make notes about the evidence source—who has done what with it—so you can see what evidence you have and how you are using it. There may be several pieces of evidence in each type (for example, Progressive Achievement Tests in Reading and Maths [PAT-R, PAT-M] and NAPLAN in formal tests). Each of these can be examined separately. The tool is a prompt to remember a range of evidence types so you can see what you have. In some cases, the boxes will be blank—these are indications of where you could take future action. Another pattern to look for is who is working with the evidence: Is it senior leaders? Do teachers, students or families engage with the evidence? What are the implications for evaluative thinking of what you find in this exercise? Who does the thinking and how is it shared?

Evidence type	Have you collected this? Systematically or informally?	Have you analysed it? Who did the analysis; what did they do?	Is it accessible now? What form is it in and who can see it? How easy is it to interpret?	Has it been used for anything? Who has used it and what for?
Results from formal tests				
Results from school-made assessments				
Exemplars or work samples				
Observations				
Surveys of students				
Surveys of families				
Surveys of staff				
Portfolios of student work				

BOX 4.1 (continued)

Evidence type	Have you collected this? Systematically or informally?	Have you analysed it? Who did the analysis; what did they do?	Is it accessible now? What form is it in and who can see it? How easy is it to interpret?	Has it been used for anything? Who has used it and what for?
Reports to parents				
Diagnostic interviews or one-to-one oral discussions				
Evidence of school culture				
Samples of in-class work				
Focus group discussions				

BOX 4.2
Types of evidence that might be important to you

- Achievement levels (In which learning areas? Level of the school? For whom?)
- Rates of progress (In which learning areas? Level of the school? For whom?)
- Equity of outcomes for groups of students
- Engagement
- Feeling of belonging
- Students' and families' feelings about school
- Families' aspirations
- Communities' aspirations
- Staff feelings and perceptions
- Development of competencies such as self-management
- Safety (emotional, cultural, behavioural)
- Problem solving
- Quality of relationships
- Wellbeing
- Creativity
- Mindsets and orientations to learning
- Confidence
- Who is accessing support, extracurricular activities and sport?

> **BOX 4.2** (continued)
> **Prompts to evaluate the evidence from your evidence audit?**
> - What do we have that would be evidence of this?
> - Is what we have 'usable' (accessible, analysed, readily interpreted)?
> - Is what we have 'useful' (aligned with our values, sound)?
> - Have we evaluated the usability and usefulness of this evidence? When?
> - What (else) could we collect that would be evidence of this in our context?

Use evaluative thinking in decision making

It is difficult to use evidence for evaluative thinking. When things are hard work it helps to have some supportive scaffolds and to practise using them. In the teacher professional learning context, it can be powerful to use a protocol that scaffolds conversation and provides opportunities to practise evaluative thinking. Protocols act as prompts, to remind people of the kind of thinking they are engaged in and provide a structure for the group that helps them move into new ways of interacting with each other. It can be difficult for people to shift the 'rules' of how they talk to each other. Providing prompt questions, or a series of steps to work through, can help them take on new ways of relating and discussing issues and evidence. The protocol in Box 4.3 is a basic example that could help you get started.

Discussing the protocol as a team and making sure it fits with your context and concerns is a good starting point. It gives people a chance to practise backing up their observations with evidence, summarising their ideas and being curious. It slows down the process of drawing conclusions so, although it may seem clunky to begin with, increasing the gap between looking at evidence and making a final judgement about it opens up a space for evaluative thinking and teacher learning.

A professional learning community leader described how things had changed in the way the group worked as a result of using the protocol to practise evaluative thinking:

> *Well, it kind of becomes your way of thinking, so when you are presented with a problem or an issue or a need for an improvement, you automatically kick into that cycle of thinking, 'Oh, okay, let's do some scanning of the evidence, and what is our goal, what are we aiming for...'*

> *It kind of just becomes the way you talk to people as well, so you say things like 'What's your hunch around that and how do you know?' or 'Maybe we can scan some evidence around that'—it kind of becomes an embedded way of having conversations with people.*
>
> Professional Learning Community Leader, K–12 school

BOX 4.3
Beginning evaluative thinking protocol

Select the sources of evidence you want to spend time interpreting (e.g. test scores, observations, student voice, informal assessment information, work samples etc.)

Ensure each team member has access to the evidence. Give them time to look at it before discussing it.

Take turns to say what you see in the evidence. Everyone has a say.

Each person summarises one key thing they see in the evidence in a minute or so. For example, 'I see that the reading scores don't change much between Year 4 and Year 5. If you look at the children's reading ages it doesn't seem there has been progress over the last 18 months for many of them.'

When each person has finished their summary, the other group members ask questions about the summary. Be careful not to make statements, or agree or disagree, just ask questions to clarify meaning. The questions could be about the summary (e.g. 'Can you tell me more about how you decided that?') or about the evidence (e.g. 'Is it the same for Year 3 to Year 4?').

The answers to the questions can be pursued as they are asked but remember that this is a time to raise questions about the summary rather than go off down rabbit holes.

The original speaker then summarises the discussion briefly by stating what they originally said and what has been discussed.

The turn passes to the next person in the group.

Interpret the evidence together

There is a difference between having evidence and interpreting it that is easy to miss. Evidence is just numbers, facts and narratives until they are interpreted and put to use for school improvement. Interpreting evidence is a skill that needs to be learned and practised. There are many different ways to interpret numerical (quantitative) evidence and non-numerical (qualitative) evidence that are beyond the scope of this book. The leadership action to be taken here is to identify someone in the school or an external facilitator who can help teachers learn how to interpret evidence, rather than assuming they will be able to do it as a matter of course.

The second part of this action is to work together in teams to learn about the interpretation of evidence. Those who interpret the evidence, understand it—quite often schools have a 'data whizz' who produces summaries for staff. This can be helpful with large datasets, but it is important that the summaries leave space for the teachers to process what it is telling them and engage with its meaning. This builds ownership and understanding of the issues revealed by the evidence. The other reason for working in groups is to support teachers who are not confident with evidence and who might be too afraid to ask for help. It also provides an opportunity to share expertise and build knowledge among staff.

A teacher who had been part of an inquiry spiral process in mathematics over a two-year period explains:

> *It definitely has changed here. It used to be top down. The leadership would tell us what the data were saying. 'This is your box and whisker plot, this is telling you that you are doing this ... this is telling you that the kids are still lagging in this area. Go and see what you can do about it.' Whereas now, there is a lot more emphasis on a PLC [professional learning community] looking at our cohort of kids and what the data is telling us. So, we actually have to go out and find out how to read a box and whisker. Not everybody knows that.*
>
> Yr 2 Teacher, K–6 school

Research in school leadership shows that leaders who participate with their staff in professional learning and inquiry processes have more success in improving outcomes for learners (Robinson et al., 2009). If school leaders work alongside their staff to look closely at evidence and to use evaluative thinking in their daily work, their schools are more likely to make changes successfully. Participating with teachers and modelling your evaluative thinking shows commitment—and it shows that these ways of working are a consistent and coherent approach at all levels of school functioning. A principal at a rural school, when talking about his school's shifts in early reading results, reflected:

> *I think a leader needs to see themselves as part of the instrument of change or as part of the team of change and not just someone on the outside.*
>
> Principal, K–8 school

Seek new forms of evidence

Many different types of evidence can be trustworthy and useful in working through student learning challenges. Policymakers often want the 'hard evidence' of standardised test scores for making educational decisions, but educators do not need to follow their lead when looking at their learners' strengths and needs. A useful concept from education research is 'triangulation'—the process by which you look at the same issue using several different types of data, to build a robust and informative picture. For example, you might look at NAPLAN scores alongside student surveys on reading and samples of work from a range of students in each class. A literacy leader describes how their school did this:

> *We interviewed the students—'What's happening for you as a learner? What works well? What can I [the teacher] do that can support you? What do I do that doesn't support you?' So, we had used NAPLAN. We had used our PAT [Progressive Achievement Test] testing, we had spoken with our students, we did work with our staff on what they were thinking, so there were lots of datasets that we collected to work out what our focus needed to be.*
>
> Yr 6 Teacher, K–8 school

The sources this teacher named each give a different type of information; taken together they build a rich picture of student learning in reading. Often there is something in the 'other', non-test evidence that schools collect that sparks engagement and action in teachers.

> *I love [that] the notion of the collection of evidence has moved beyond test results, so we're asking about kids' attitude and things, and that gave us a lot of valuable information.*
>
> Deputy Principal, K–6 school

Hearing directly from the students about their perceptions of school, learning and teaching, and giving them the opportunity to comment on the evidence about them, can be extremely valuable. It also engages them in the whole process of inquiry and using evidence in evaluative thinking. In our work in Australian schools, hearing from students has proven to be the greatest catalyst for change.

Gathering multiple perspectives has several benefits: it makes people question their assumptions, it may lead to fresh insights or ideas for action, it gives everyone involved an understanding of the evidence, and it makes people discuss their perspectives and ideas using evidence as a base.

Another highly valuable source of evidence for leading of professional learning is evidence of teaching practice. This evidence can take many forms, such as observations by another teacher, videos of teaching, reflections by teachers or student surveys. None of these sources of evidence by themselves provide sufficient information—it is essential to interpret and discuss what the evidence reveals. Observations, for example, provide a direct record of practice, but they are framed by what the observer is focusing on and notices. Observations are most useful if they are jointly constructed by the teacher and the observer and use a protocol for discussing the lesson afterwards (e.g. Timperley, 2014). Observations can be peer-to-peer or undertaken by school leaders, depending on the purpose and use of the resultant evidence. Teachers' reflections or lesson evaluations and notes might be useful sources of evidence, and student voice on teaching has proved to be a rich source of information about the effectiveness of different practices (MET Project, 2013). Through the spiral of inquiry process, evaluative thinking calls on us to ask about the impact of any actions. Evidence about what those actions are needs to be considered alongside evidence about the impacts of the actions. Real shifts in practice come when the links between teacher practice and student outcomes are carefully explored.

Link evidence of student learning with changes in teaching, leadership and organisational practices

A substantial challenge in using evidence and evaluative thinking to work on student learning issues in schools is linking evidence of student learning with changes in teaching, leadership and organisational practices. When this happens, decisions can be made about what to retain and what to change. At times, evidence of teaching, leadership and organisational practices may be thin on the ground but, without making links between these layers, it will be difficult to make real progress in improving student outcomes.

One way to think about linking evidence types is to plan to deliberately collect evidence from multiple layers. The Planning for Evidence Gathering Tool in Box 4.4 is a way to tackle this task. The tool also encourages coherence between parts of the school system by asking the inquiry teams to identify explicitly those changes that will impact the student learning focus, making it clear if proposed activities are aligned with the focus or not.

BOX 4.4
Planning for Evidence Gathering Tool

What evidence will you gather to monitor the extent to which the changes in practice and outcomes for students are happening and progress is being made towards the goals and targets you have developed?

First, list the student outcomes you want and the associated teaching practices, leadership practices and organisational practices that you think will support these student outcomes. This list should describe the position that you want to be in once the changes have taken place.

Students' learning and engagement: ....
Teaching practice(s): ....
Leadership practice(s): ....
Organisational practice(s): ....

Area of intended change and outcomes	Baseline What does the evidence tell us about what is happening?	After 1 Term What changes will we expect to see and how will we know?	After 2 Terms What changes will we expect to see and how will we know?	After 3 Terms What changes will we expect to see and how will we know?
Student learning and engagement				
Changes in teaching practice				
Changes in leadership practice				

First, the team using this tool need to identify the student learning need that is the focus of inquiry and work out what can be collected as evidence of change in the focus area. How much change do they expect to see? Over what time frame? Then they need to work out what teaching, leadership and organisational practices will need to change in order to realise the change in student learning. For example, if a K–6 school is trying to improve numeracy, teachers may need to use more manipulatives and group their students differently, longer sessions for mathematics may need to be programmed, leaders may need to co-teach in classrooms, and regular staff meetings might need to be given over to looking at student work and discussing next steps.

To use the tool described in Box 4.4, begin with the current state, using information gathered during scanning what is going on for learners. Use the grid to record the current, baseline state for students, teachers, leaders and the school as an organisation in relation to your student learning focus. Working from this learning focus, think about what changes in teaching practice might be needed to bring about the identified changes in student learning. Next, think about how leaders' practice might need to change to support the teachers to enact the new practices you have identified. Finally, think about the ways that organisational practices might be constraining leaders and teachers from enacting the new practices or might be opening up opportunities for new practice to emerge.

Then, discuss and record what changes will be observable after one, two and three terms at each layer of the school: teachers, leaders and organisation. The question, 'What changes would we expect to see and how will we know?' reminds everyone of the need to find sources of evidence of change, and to plan ahead for what these will be, to identify the impact of the changes. 'What would it look like if this change had taken place?' can be a helpful discussion starter for identifying sources of evidence that change has occurred.

This tool can be revisited each term to see if the predicted changes have been made, and to alter future expectations based on what is observed. When you revisit the tool, also review the links you proposed between the layers and see if you made some assumptions that proved to be incorrect. For example, you may have decided that teachers needed to be given new resources in order to make changes to their practice, but in reality, supplying the new resource has not led to the changes you anticipated.

Give it time and keep coming back to it

Overnight success cannot be expected with something as complex as using evidence and evaluative thinking. The process of change is rarely incremental. Things may not change for a long time, and then suddenly they seem to change all at once. There may be lots of energy for change in some parts of a school, but not so much elsewhere. Teachers may make some substantial shifts and then seem to fall back into old ways again. These are all typical and unavoidable characteristics of working with people and working with long-term, complex problems. Taking a long view is important, along with recognising 'wins' when you get them, and giving time for the process to unfold. This does not mean allowing things to grind to a halt, but rather investigating what is happening if things are not changing.

Rachel, deputy principal at a K–6 school, talks about the time it has taken for teachers to be able to engage with evidence or data without feeling blamed for it:

> *That has been a bit of a journey. So, when I first started this, that was four years ago, there was a lot of conversation around data but we had to read or look at the data and remove the blame. When we look at the data it's about where the children are at, and I used to say this all the time: 'This is not about you, this is about what the children are doing and how we are going to make it better. I don't really care what's gone on in the past, except we will use that to learn how to improve'. And we got a few small wins with literacy, so we were able to move forward. There was a lot of testing and not a lot of analysis—but as soon as we could paint a picture from the data, then there was an acceptance of the data and we were able to move.*
>
> *Deputy Principal, K–6 school*

The other way in which you need to 'give it time' is to allow time for the conversations and knowledge building that needs to occur among staff members. Allowing time out from classrooms to collaborate and move work forward signals respect for the task that the teachers are doing. Cutting down on other work, other meetings and other foci helps too—create time and space for the teachers to use evidence and practise evaluative thinking.

These opportunities cannot be one-off events or something that happens at the beginning and end of the year. Evaluative thinking is a mindset that pervades the way schools and the educators within them work on improving teaching and learning, and so using evidence is a process that occurs throughout school life. In the end it will become a habit, but as the school learns to work in this way, time and space for coming back to evidence will build evaluative thinking. As this leader describes:

> *You are always going back and rechecking and seeing where you are going. Without evidence you are just another person with an opinion.*
>
> *Deputy Principal, K–6 school*

Using a spiral model of inquiry emphasises that professional learning does not end, and that returning to the evidence is a central part of working out 'Where are we at?' and 'Where to next?'

> *The spiral challenges you to go back to the evidence, reflect on what's working and what's not, and keep moving forward.*
> Deputy Principal, K–6 school

Returning to evidence also provides a space for acknowledging and celebrating progress. If evidence is not used to check where things are at, no-one will see the progress made. Tessa describes how important this was in her school:

> *Having a clear focus, a goal that actually directed you where you were going to and then checking if you were getting there—I think those targets are really important because when you manage to achieve those targets it unifies people who struggle through it and kind of convinces them that it's worth going again, and you can kind of have a celebration—I think it's really important.*
> Professional Learning Community Leader, K–12 school

Conclusion

Using evidence and evaluative thinking are two fundamental elements in making change in schools and improving outcomes for learners. They are related to each other, as evaluative thinking uses evidence to make decisions and to consider the impact of practice. To build evaluative thinking as an approach to challenges in schools, teachers and leaders need to be confident selectors, collectors, organisers and analysts of a range of evidence types. Once they have good evidence to consider, they also need to know how to work out what it says and what it means for future practice. These are all important skills that will be distributed among a staff of teachers, rather than belonging just to one or two experts. Some skills may need to be explicitly taught by specialists or facilitators. Supporting professional learning that builds familiarity with evidence and how to use it to make decisions is a major contribution that leaders can make to improving outcomes for the learners in their schools.

CHAPTER 5
Equity, bias and beliefs

The challenge

Educational equity is widely discussed, not well understood, frequently avoided and challenging to achieve—all of which perpetuate existing inequity. Despite successive government policies such as Closing the Gap and the National Indigenous English Literacy and Numeracy Strategy, along with the more recent Australian Professional Standard for Principals (AITSL, 2015), Australia has an education system where some groups of students, especially non-Indigenous students and those in the independent school sector, achieve better than others in scientific, reading and mathematical literacy domains (Thomson, De Bortoli, & Underwood, 2016). This inequity is 'a long-standing, seemingly intractable issue, regularly announced and denounced in policy, media and educational circles' (Kenway, 2013, p. 286).

In this chapter we explore the concept of equity, and how bias, based on our beliefs and experiences, can be a powerful contributor to making equity difficult to achieve. We consider how understanding more about biases, especially those that we are unaware of, may be a powerful starting place for leaders to deliberately address inequitable outcomes in their classrooms and schools.

Equity matters because failure at school penalises learners for life. There is clear evidence that equity in education pays off; an equitable education system can compensate for broader social and economic inequities by strengthening economic growth and social wellbeing (OECD, 2012). Equity is about fairness and inclusion where fairness ensures that personal and social circumstances, such as gender, ethnicity and family background, are not obstacles to success (OECD, 2012). Inequity occurs when there are consistent differences in outcomes for groups of learners.

This issue of how bias may contribute to issues of equity is illustrated in a recent New Zealand study involving over 11 000 students (Meissel et al., 2017). When asked to make an overall judgement of writing achievement, teachers judged girls to be better writers than boys even when their standardised test scores were the same. The effect was compounded when the boys were from ethnic minority groups. As one teacher accurately reflected:

> *So, if it's a European girl getting the same score on the standardised test as the Maori or Pasifika boy, the overall teacher judgement is much lower for the Maori or Pasifika boy than the girl.*
>
> Yr 6 Teacher, F–6 school

This effect applied irrespective of school size or the socio-economic level of the community. The implications are that, if teachers judge some students to be poorer writers than their actual achievement indicates, then the academic challenge of the work presented to them is likely to be much lower, thus limiting their opportunities to learn. When teacher judgements are based on perceptions rather than evidence, they create significant barriers to educational achievement, particularly for Indigenous learners (Forrest, Lean, & Dunn, 2016). Taking action to challenge these biases and the beliefs that feed them offers a promising vehicle for change.

The reason why this is a challenge

All educators want to make a positive difference for the students they teach. At the same time, everyone has biases that drive how they make sense of the world. For leaders and teachers, these biases influence how schools are organised and how students are taught. Our biases are typically so much a part of how we see the world and perceive others that we are mostly unaware we have them—they are unconscious. Unconscious bias occurs when an 'individual automatically or unconsciously classifies a person as a member of a group, applies stereotypes to the others based on their group membership, and makes decisions based on these stereotypes' (Blank, Hokomau, & Kingi, 2016, p. 13). This is particularly common for members of a dominant group or culture because these biases are continually reinforced and perpetuated by the environment.

Biases influence judgements through what is noticed, and they inform decision making and actions. Leaders and teachers must make multiple decisions throughout the school day and beyond. Most of these in-the-moment decisions are based on tacit knowledge and perceptions of learners with unconscious bias playing a part when deciding what to teach to whom. They influence expectations. This works favourably for those learners who experience high expectations from their teachers but impacts negatively for those who experience low expectations, as this newly appointed principal explained:

> *It was really obvious to me that there were beliefs in this school that need[ed] to be surfaced before any professional learning is going to make any significant change. The teacher discussion was, 'Our kids are two-year kids—they take two years to complete one'. So that's about beliefs and low expectations.*
>
> *Principal, F–6 school*

Biases are difficult to address, both in the classroom and beyond. This is, in part, because most people are unaware of them, do not fully understand how they work and, understandably, reject the idea that they hold them because they want the best for their students. It is difficult to address something that we are not consciously aware of and that our daily experiences may unknowingly reinforce. This school leader understood some of the complexity:

> *Sometimes we only think culture is there when it is visible. There are many things that are visible and there are a heap more ... [where] it's not visible and sometimes all of those assumptions that we make about that, you know. Sometimes the subtleties of culture are not as evident because you can't see, as I am looking from where I look and I might miss something completely from somebody else's point of view.*
>
> *Deputy Principal, Yr 7–12 school*

Unconscious bias can contribute to the current and longstanding inequity of outcomes. One of the challenges in addressing equity, however, is that it is confused with equality. Equality is primarily about sameness or difference (inequality), which leads to teaching practices that provide equal access to resources and knowledge where 'learners are treated the same'. This idea of sameness frequently ignores learner's cultural identity (McKenzie & Phillips, 2016). In reality, these situations do not provide equal opportunities to learn because these opportunities are influenced by the dominant culture of schools to which different students have differential access. Despite this issue, lack of success of some students is often blamed on learners' lack of effort, their family background or both, ignoring any underlying historical and current inequity. To address the issue, different opportunities are needed for many of these students to have the same opportunities to access the curriculum. This idea is

FIGURE 5.1: Equality and equity
Source: Interaction Institute for Social Change. Artist: Angus Maguire (developed from an image by Craig Froehle).

simply, but powerfully, illustrated in Figure 5.1. Just as the shorter child needs a box to see what others are seeing, so do many students need help to 'see' what the teachers see.

Leadership actions to address the challenge

Good intention is rarely enough to challenge the problematic underlying biases that maintain the status quo of inequitable outcomes. Six leadership actions that challenge inequity are explained in the following section.

Examine equity policies and systems

Reviewing school equity policies begins by understanding the meaning of equity and how it is different from equality. Such a review is only beneficial, however, if it influences thinking and actions. Purposefully thinking about equity makes us consider how the school is addressing inequity for disadvantaged groups and what forces are perpetuating inequitable outcomes. Achieving equity may require time to understand the historical background of biases that impact on inequity of outcomes for students and identifying where these biases play out in current policies, systems and practices.

It is difficult to identify our own biases because of their unconscious nature. One possibility to counteract this problem when reviewing policies and school practices is to develop deeper connections and authentic partnerships with learners and their families (Hynds et al., 2016). Conversations that unpack students' past experiences of schooling and their current experiences of 'this school' may provide insights into cultural mismatches between home and how students experience school, especially for students from communities that differ from our own. When having such conversations, it is important to bring an appreciative lens towards the cultural resources the students and their families bring to these conversations and the school. What cultural capital and experiences do these families bring that can be utilised in how the school is organised and what is taught? How could this knowledge shape the policies and systems of our school? How can this knowledge lead to a shared vision of learning and change, and improved equity in outcomes?

Promoting equity and excellence is a challenging and, at times, uncomfortable task. The strong forces of the status quo mean that nothing less than an unrelenting and deliberate focus by leaders on both equity and excellence will be needed to embed them in the school culture. Equity and excellence both need to be visible and explicit in policies and systems within a school, as a starting place for action. Leaders can use the questions in Box 5.1 to check that their policies, systems, processes and decision making support equity as a first step towards embedding them in the school culture.

BOX 5.1
Possible equity questions: Policies, systems, processes and decision making

With your leadership team ask:
1. What is our deliberate vision for inclusiveness in our school?
2. How do our policies value each learner's identity, culture and language?
3. How do we deliberately consider bias in our policies, systems and decision making?
4. How do we deliberately collaborate and engage with the diverse voices in the community in our decision making?
5. What evaluative protocols and probes do we use to check our impact for equity? What do we do as a result?
6. Do we provide 'special' solutions that inadvertently exclude or limit future choices and outcomes?

Develop knowledge of how unconscious bias works

Biases help us categorise and make sense of the the world. They are especially influential in quick or automatic decision making. In his best-selling book, *Thinking fast and slow*, Daniel Kahneman (2011) explains the two systems we all use to make sense of the world. System 1 is fast, intuitive (gut feelings) and operates outside conscious awareness. It functions from an affective and experiential memory base allowing bias (positive and negative) to play a powerful part in determining our actions and decisions. System 2 is slower, more deliberate, conscious and potentially more 'rational'. This is when we stop and think.

But much of our thinking uses System 1 as we would struggle with the cognitive load required to process the world at the slower speed of System 2. System 1 thinking kicks in when there is ambiguous and incomplete evidence, when there are time constraints and within subjective situations, such as when we make judgements about effort and behaviour. It comes to the fore particularly when we are busy and stressed. The biases that drive System 1 thinking help us fill in the gaps to make sense of a situation. We probably do not even notice or connect our actions to bias. As such, unconscious bias cannot be disconnected or turned off at will when we make these quick decisions. These decisions can be the opposite of our conscious intentions. Figure 5.2 is an image that has been used when working with school leaders in order to prompt consideration of possible unconscious bias and the assumptions we make. Box 5.2 contains prompts and questions relating to the figure that can be used in your own work.

We form biases from everything we see and experience throughout our lives. Biases are influenced at the societal level, where existing norms and ways of being are taken for granted. The news media play an influential role, especially around promoting deficit discourse about ethnic groups. Indigenous Australians, some migrant groups and their cultures are frequently framed as

BOX 5.2
Assessing our unconscious biases
- Look at Figure 5.2. for 10 seconds. Think of three words that come to mind.
- What if you knew this man was a teacher committed to equity returning home after an exhausting day? Think of three words.
- When you have more 'story' and slow your thinking down, do you have the same words and reach the same conclusion?

FIGURE 5.2: Interrupting our meaning making
Source: Image by Nick Twyford

a problem. These negative stereotypes reinforce the acceptance of the failure of these groups. It is not surprising that one in 10 Australians (1.5 million of the nation's adult population) believe that some races are inferior or superior to others despite 46 per cent of Australians having at least one parent born overseas (Australian Human Rights Commission, 2014).

> The problem is in the way we frame these issues. We're all caught in this thing called a 'deficit discourse' and we don't even know we're in it ... however, all the thinking and the assumptions underneath this framing is really subtle and mostly out of people's awareness (Gorringe, 2015, para. 1 and 4).

The way history is taught, and talked about, also informs the way people think—which informs unconscious, and possibly conscious, bias. For example, historical education policies have led to the deficit framing of Indigenous Peoples as 'less able to learn' than non-Indigenous (Sarra, Spillman, Jackson, Davis, & Bray, 2018). These negatively framed policies are believed to still contribute to low expectations of Indigenous learners by some educators. Policy maintains these views through 'deficit accounts that attribute blame to "disadvantaged groups"' (Sarra et al., 2018, p. 1). As a result, strategies are implemented that focus on Indigenous learners needing to 'catch up', which, 'in turn may reinforce these assumptions with teachers and society at large and most likely Indigenous peoples themselves leading to students' negative cultural identity' (Sarra et al., 2018, p. 3). This results in blaming of students and their families for their lack of educational success. Rather, the emphasis needs to be less on problems of dysfunction and remedying deficits, and more on identifying opportunities and realising potential. Similar examples can be found for many other groups of diverse learners.

Use inquiry and evidence to check for and challenge bias and inequity

An effective way to check for bias and inequity is to deliberately use inquiry and evidence to uncover the systems, processes and practices that maintain inequity. No-one is likely to accept, or even consider, changing their beliefs without convincing evidence that the alternative is either worthwhile or that there exists incontestable evidence against the existing belief (Timperley & Robinson, 2001).

Undertaking a thorough audit of school policies and practices that checks for inherent disadvantage and advantage is also essential. This means slowing down to System 2 thinking and collaborating with those who may bring different perspectives. Having systems in place to check for the presence of bias can lead to many 'Aha' moments as educators come to terms with their possible bias that may get in the way when working with diverse learners, as this school leader described:

> *Get that inquiry happening—do that at leadership level, do it at team level, do it at teacher level in all of those places so it's personal and so we can start talking about this child in relationship to who they really are and what they might have in mind, you know ... the difference between what we think and what is actually there because sometimes you can assume about the kids that ... they don't know something or they are not interested in education or their parents aren't interested in education and those sorts of things.*
>
> *School Leader, K–6 School*

The use of the spiral of inquiry (see the Introduction) or similar frameworks and tools are useful places to support this audit. These frameworks help to bring beliefs and biases to the surface. The spiral of inquiry begins by asking 'What is going on for our learners?' in the scanning phase. The intention is to find out about their experience of school, not only from an academic perspective, but also from cultural and social-emotional perspectives. Do they feel they belong? Who believes they will be a success in life? By asking the students and their families about what is happening for them from their perspective, leaders and teachers can begin to understand how a school's systems and processes may disadvantage particular students.

The 'hunch' phase is another stage to deliberately look at how the actions of leaders and teachers are impacting on the experience of learners. Listening for beliefs that create bias, such as blaming of students or their families without checking with evidence, is paramount here. This can be uncomfortable as participants are asked to challenge their own deep-seated beliefs, and especially challenging if the evidence disputes these long-held beliefs. As a school leader shared:

> *We used to always say that the students couldn't read because there were no books at home and the parents didn't care. When we checked we found that parents really cared and wanted their children to be lawyers and doctors and bought their children books but didn't really know how to work with them to teach them to read. We had never talked to them about helping their children learn to read because we thought they would do it wrong.*
>
> *Principal, F–8 school*

Box 5.3 suggests a list of questions that interrogate how evidence is interpreted from an equity perspective. These questions can be used with the whole staff as prompts for discussion about how evidence is used and can identify places where changes can be made to reduce sources of bias and make more equitable resource and evidence-based decisions.

In schools and classrooms, equity is about the attitudes of teachers and fellow students who either promote or inhibit a climate of equity (Ainscow, 2016) because this is a key way that systemic sources of inequity play out in people's lives. Ignoring problematic beliefs is not an option for improvement, the major challenge for school leaders is to engage them in ways that challenge and change them, and inquiry processes provide a structured way to do this.

> **BOX 5.3**
> **Possible equity questions: Interpreting evidence**
> With your staff ask:
> 1. Are we more effective with some groups of students?
> 2. How do we develop each learner's identity, culture and language? What do our learners and their families say?
> 3. Do we expect and accept differences in groups of learners' results?
> 4. Do we make assumptions and judgements with insufficient evidence or from limited examples?
> 5. Do we look for confirming evidence to prove our thinking?
> 6. Do we ask each other to give evidence to support our thinking?
> 7. Do we slow down our thinking to limit bias?
> 8. Do we collaborate when we interpret evidence? Do we allow others to help us see different points of view?

Surface and process problematic biases and beliefs

Schools, through their leaders, have an opportunity to challenge and disrupt problematic and discriminatory beliefs that fuel bias. Ignoring bias allows the beliefs to remain unchecked and continue to flourish, thereby influencing policies, decision making and actions that maintain and legitimise inequity (Francis, Mills, & Lupton, 2017). Taking action starts with surfacing our own unconscious bias into conscious awareness, otherwise everyone will continue to 'use their own unexamined frames of reference against which to judge students, students' families, and their communities' (Sleeter, 2008, p. 561).

The Implicit Association Test is an online test that provides test-takers with feedback on their unconscious or implicit bias (see https://implicit.harvard.edu/implicit/). The test highlights the differences between our conscious thoughts and unconscious biases on associations we may have on social attitudes (e.g. race, gender and sexual orientation) and mental health (e.g. self-esteem, anxiety and alcohol). Test-takers are often surprised and uncomfortable to learn they respond differently when thinking about 'different others'.

So what next? After raising awareness of the existence of bias, it is necessary to continue to do something to minimise its impact. In addition to using inquiry processes to work from evidence rather than assumptions, you can openly name and discuss bias and beliefs, and check how they affect your actions and decisions. You can attend to everyday interactions, such as humour based on gender, ability or ethnicity; question assumptions that are held by teachers, learners, their families and wider community as they arise; and highlight negative messaging in the media. Deliberate 'evidence checking' assumptions about students and how they learn, and ensuring expectations remain high for all students, are useful strategies for surfacing and processing problematic biases and beliefs. Critical self-reflection helps raise any unconscious bias to the surface where the bias can be checked for impact or discrepancies with intentions. The questions in Box 5.4 below can be used to support self-reflection. Noticing bias and privilege can be difficult for members of a dominant group who are surrounded by their own values and culture, making their culture invisible to them. Colleagues from different cultures can, in inclusive school cultures with a safe environment, make these assumptions more visible by sharing their everyday experiences of discrimination to enable others to see their realities.

> **BOX 5.4**
> **Possible equity questions for self-reflection: Bias and beliefs**
> 1. How do I think about equity in my school and my community?
> 2. Do I hold different expectations for different groups of students?
> 3. Do I believe that success is mostly about individual effort? Is this possible if the system itself is currently deficit?
> 4. Do I locate the problem of low achievement within the child and their families?
> 5. Do I believe in 'special' solutions for learners rather than tailoring education to the student?
> 6. Do I treat everyone the same?
> 7. How do I respond to problematic actions on the part of teachers, students or in the community? Do I walk away? What makes me do this?

Working with bias and problematic beliefs requires leaders to be courageous as these conversations are often uncomfortable, especially if this is a new way of working. An inclusive learning culture and the use of protocols can make it safe to contest beliefs in ways that are non-judgemental of past decisions and actions.

> *Now we are co-constructing each phase of the spiral of inquiry with them ... so they feel safe to confront their own practice, beliefs and make changes because they know that they're not going to be criticised. It's actually about problem solving together I think. It's taking that approach.*
> *Principal, P–6 school*

Deprivatise practice

Biases and beliefs make everyone susceptible to noticing only things that work to confirm their existing thinking and lead to blindspots in practice—it is difficult to know what we do that could be improved. Observers, with prior training and guiding protocols, are more likely to see the blindspots we can not and help us address the actions that get in the way of promoting equitable outcomes.

If leaders open up their practice first, it can demonstrate to teachers the necessity of deprivatising practice to make unconscious bias visible. Leaders who are willing to be open to this kind of scrutiny are usually respected by their teachers. In this way, leaders communicate high expectations of themselves, their teachers and their students, and build an inclusive learning culture where inquiry, challenge and support enhance improvement efforts. Once leaders open up their practice, it is also important to check if any differences are changing the expectations teachers have of students.

Take affirmative, strengths-based action

Affirmative action means replacing deficit beliefs with high-expectation learning environments (Stronger Smarter Institute, 2014) and implementing preferential treatments or unequal distribution of resources to enable all students to succeed (Ishimaru & Galloway, 2014). Remember the small child on the box in Figure 5.1? What kind of boxes do some of your students need for them to be successful? Taking affirmative action and using affirmative frameworks recognises, values and celebrates the richness and diversity in school communities, their languages and cultures. Leaders can shift their own and others' thinking to believe that all learners—Indigenous, multi-cultural, multi-faith, at-risk and those with differing needs—can become creative, confident, active, informed learners and citizens given the opportunity (AITSL, 2015). Problematic beliefs are discussed and replaced with new knowledge and understanding gained through inquiry-based professional learning. Are students whose first language is not English seen to be a problem, or are the total language resources they bring seen as a strength? Educational resources such as the website Your Story, Our Journey (see www.yourstoryourjourney.net) help educators engage with Aboriginal and Torres Strait Islander parents and caregivers.

> *We need to treat all language as valid because it might be the valued language of the home so we need to think about how we make*

> *connections with that variety or dialect of English and standard school English rather than saying you're not allowed to talk like that here, so it just was a light bulb [moment]. I used to continually correct this little boy. I did not take into account the importance of his own language — he speaks how he writes, he writes how he speaks, this is his language. This is what he's bringing in from home. For so long not speaking good classroom English has been seen as a deficit.*
>
> Teacher, P–6 school

Implicit in this idea is building, not only tolerance but acceptance and, eventually, enjoyment, of difference.

Conclusion

Bias and beliefs drive actions. Schooling based on historical and unconscious biases works well for many learners, but systematically disadvantages others. School leaders play a key role in challenging the status quo and seeking continuous improvement, especially in areas like equity, which can be sensitive and difficult to deal with (AITSL, 2015). Raising awareness of, and explicitly challenging problematic bias and beliefs, requires leaders to embark on an ongoing, deliberate journey. This work is complex and there is no quick fix. It is immersed in seen and unseen emotion, vulnerability and risk. It requires courageous leadership underpinned by inquiry, evaluative thinking and an unwavering belief in social justice. It also requires an inclusive learning culture that provides opportunities for all staff to learn and improve together, in a safe space where the focus is on 'how will we do better' (AITSL, 2015). Affirmative action goes beyond the school gates into the wider political sphere where biases and beliefs influence such things as policy design and resourcing, which, in turn, impact on equity. Educators have a role in challenging the systemic causes of inequity as well as dealing with the impacts of bias on individual students' lives. Addressing unconscious bias and beliefs provides a means to change views and practices in the journey to reach equity and excellence for all in education.

CHAPTER 6
Extended examples

In this book we have outlined five key challenges for school leaders who are trying to create learning-focused school environments, where inquiry mindsets predominate and outcomes for learners are improving. In each chapter we have suggested leadership actions that address these five challenges, describing each of them and giving tools and examples to help leaders understand how they work.

In reality, both the challenges and the leadership actions are not as clear-cut as we have described here. In busy, complex school contexts, particular events will raise more than one challenge at a time, and one leadership action might impact several challenges—indeed, leadership actions that impact several challenges are high leverage and very useful. To give a sense of how the challenges and leadership actions might play out in context, this chapter provides two extended examples—one from a primary school and one from a secondary school. In each case the school leadership are attempting an inquiry spiral-based approach to improving outcomes for learners and to teacher professional learning. Both schools get off to a shaky start, but they learn from this and reapproach the spiral of inquiry in a new way.

This chapter might be useful as a way to understand the spiral, some typical challenges faced by schools doing this kind of work and the leadership actions we have suggested. It could serve either as an introduction to the ideas or as a summary. It might be helpful to use the examples as the basis for a discussion among leadership team members or staff. Some of the leadership actions suggested in the previous chapters are exemplified in these two descriptions. Looking for these and discussing them with colleagues might be a way to deepen your understanding of what the leadership actions might look like in practice.

HILLY PRIMARY

Context and getting started

Hilly Primary School is a K–7 school in a rural town. It has 14 classroom teachers, and a principal and deputy principal without class responsibilities. There are two part-time teachers who cover teacher release and some small group teaching, as well as six teacher aides who support special needs students in the classroom and run the library and resource room. The teachers have always worked in three teams: junior, middle and senior. Each of these teams has a strong leader, with different priorities and strategies for learning. Hilly Primary's current principal (Jenny) arrived at the beginning of the previous year. Last year passed in a bit of a whirl as she came to terms with Hilly Primary and its staff, trying to understand what was happening and why.

Hilly Primary is in a less affluent part of town. Aboriginal and Torres Strait Islander students make up seven per cent of the school's roll. Recently, a number of refugee families have been resettled in the area and immigrant workers have arrived to help on local farms. Hilly Primary now has more linguistic and cultural diversity than it has experienced in the past and several of the refugee children have suffered severe trauma in their home countries.

Hilly Primary has a supportive parent group that raises money for the school, but there are also a number of parents who are not engaged with the school at the moment. Some of the engaged parents are critical of the school in the community and have a Facebook group where comments about teachers and, sometimes, students are published. Some parents have started to move their children to Flats Primary, on the other side of town, where they perceive there are fewer disruptive students and better academic results.

Hilly Primary has always had disappointing NAPLAN results, especially in mathematics, where the school averages are well below state averages for all year groups. Progress between Years 3 to 5 were all in the 'red'. Progress in reading is better; writing is in between. The school has generally put poor progress down to having a difficult group of students with high social needs and low concentration spans. The local high school, which most of Hilly Primary's students go on to, has a very low opinion of Hilly Primary's teaching, particularly in mathematics. They feel that Hilly Primary students are inadequately prepared for high school mathematics and are set up to fail from the beginning.

As a new year begins, Jenny is ready to start tackling some of the issues related to student outcome and teacher practice that she has observed. She is aware that if she imposes changes, they will not 'stick'. She also knows the importance of developing evaluative thinking for making sustained change in schools, so she has decided to use the spiral of inquiry to guide the staff through a process of professional learning. Jenny's principal at her last school had used the spiral of inquiry with success, and she thinks it is an engaging and supportive way to work with her staff on the issues she has noticed.

First attempt at an inquiry approach

At the first staff meeting of the year, Jenny invites the staff to work with her to decide on a focus for their professional learning for the year. She lets the staff know that they will be working together on one school-wide focus, beginning from what the students need. This is a big change for the staff, who are used to individually choosing their own workshops each year to attend and pursuing their own interests. They are also not used to working as a whole staff because the main meeting forum has been teams, with whole staff meetings being infrequent and used for administration. The team leaders feel usurped and undermined, even though Jenny discussed it with them earlier on, and they do not respond much in the staff meeting apart from insisting that the teachers discuss what the focus should be in teams and report back, rather than mixing up the year levels. The teachers readily agree.

The discussion is supposed to be based on scanning the evidence that the school already has about its students and seeing if there are significant patterns or issues that emerge. Jenny has prepared some information for them to work with: graphic summaries of NAPLAN data, PAT-M and PAT-R scores, summaries of a survey of engagement and attitudes to school, some feedback from last year's school council students and notes from the last parent group meeting about issues the parents raised. At Jenny's request, the teachers have also brought their computers with class data on and their reports from last year that contain information about a broader range of subjects.

As the discussion begins, Jenny notices that the computers are closed and the set of paper documents she has provided remains untouched—but there is plenty of talk as the teachers share their ideas about what is 'wrong'. At the end of the session, the junior school have identified oral language as their key issue, the middle school have settled on spelling and the senior school are concerned about engagement and behaviour. Each group has a number of reasons why the focus of the other groups is not appropriate for them. None of the groups refers to the evidence.

Jenny has some choices to make. She wants the teachers to engage with using the spiral of inquiry, and maybe pursuing their chosen issues will be helpful with getting their cooperation. On the other hand, Jenny believes that having a shared focus will be more productive and might bring the staff together. She needs to find a place to start building the staff's evaluative thinking. Both of these options will do that and, because the spiral is non-linear, there will be opportunities to come back to the focus as the work progresses.

After the meeting, each of the team leaders comes to see her, one by one. They are all very sure that their staff will not buy into a school-wide focus and that they should be allowed to pursue the challenges they have identified, which they claim are long term and critical. Jenny is torn; she knows from her reading that they should share the focus and work together and that the ideas are not based on looking at the evidence she provided.

She also knows they haven't asked the students about their experience of school, but everyone is already so angry about the changes that perhaps a compromise is needed. She agrees with the team leaders. They meet together and talk about the next steps. Jenny shares a reading about the inquiry spiral with the team leaders and they discuss interviewing students and then focusing on a key area that combines the evidence they already have with what the students are telling them. Teams meet weekly, so the team leaders agree to meet Jenny again in a month and report back about what happened.

In early March, the team leaders and Jenny get together to talk about their inquiries. Each of the team leaders talks at length about the challenges posed by the students and their attitudes, and the students' parents. There seems to be little progress from the first staff meeting in January. The team leaders explain how beginning of the year busyness has meant lots of admin time in meetings, and not much time to advance the inquiry discussion. Jenny is disappointed but recognises how busy the beginning of the year is, so they set a new date and agree to meet then.

Unfortunately, the meeting gets postponed because two of the team leaders are away from school on a sports exchange, so it is near the end of Term 1 when they can talk again. At this meeting it becomes clear that there has been little or no progress during Term 1. Again, the leaders are clear about the problems they and their teachers experience with students and parents, sharing anecdotes about angry parents disturbing classes, extreme oppositional behaviour from students and children forgetting their books and not bringing them in each day. Jenny feels almost like these problems are being given to her to deal with, when what she had intended was a collaborative, whole-school professional learning experience that used everyone's expertise. She decides to try again in Term 2.

Scanning

On the last day of the holidays before Term 2 starts, Jenny calls an all-day staff meeting. She invites an outside facilitator who has worked with the spiral of inquiry in other schools to help her lead the learning with her staff. Jenny feels that having outside knowledge and expertise may help the teachers to engage with the spiral process because an 'outsider' may be able to press on the teachers' ideas more strongly than she can. The facilitator introduces the basic concepts and provides an overview of the inquiry spiral process. Then Jenny provides the teachers with the evidence she prepared for the January meeting, along with beginning of the year testing results, and the facilitator groups the teachers in cross-team groups.

With the support of the facilitator, Jenny guides the teachers to consider the evidence and to work from the student experience 'up' to the inquiry focus. The facilitator suggests a key question for the teachers to use as they discuss the evidence—he has written it on cards and given one to each group. The question is a prompt to keep the teachers focused on the evidence they have, not on anecdotes or untested beliefs: 'What evidence supports that idea?' The question becomes a bit of a running joke in the meeting, with teachers using it when Jenny announces that it is morning teatime; but they are using it with each other too and getting into the spirit of linking their statements to the evidence.

They pay particular attention to the difference in the reading and maths NAPLAN data because they find that interesting. Jenny and the facilitator can hear that the conversation is broadening out from last term's concerns and becoming more focused on the learners' experiences. There are 'grumblers', however, some checking phones and replying to emails while others won't let go of last term's ideas and keep trying to bring the conversation back to the Term 1 topics.

As the discussion proceeds, the engaged teachers and the 'grumblers' start to both say the same thing for different reasons: 'We don't have the right data/enough data to understand some of the trends we see'. Jenny picks up on this, she acknowledges there are grumblings and leads a discussion about what additional data are needed and how they might get these. The facilitator suggests that maybe looking at target learners might be better than trying to gather large amounts of additional data from the whole school, which will be time-consuming to get and hard to process. By the end of the day, the staff have agreed to interview three students in each class (one who achieves well, one who is struggling and one whose first language is not English) about their learning, especially in reading and mathematics because of the difference in NAPLAN. The interview questions were: 'Do you know what it means to be a successful reader?', 'Do you know how you are going in your reading?' and 'Do you know what to do next to improve your reading?' These questions were repeated for maths.

Jenny knows things are starting to change when two of the teachers come separately to her office. The first one is Sandra from the senior school. She had found the students' responses so interesting that she had interviewed half the class. She talks about how the higher achieving students found maths boring compared with reading and didn't like doing lots of examples when they understood the key ideas already. In contrast, the lower achieving and second language students could answer the questions reasonably well for reading but struggled to do so in mathematics. They seemed to understand maths as learning basic facts and getting the right answer but described successful readers as understanding what they were reading. Sandra could see why the students thought this from differences in the way she taught these students in the two learning areas.

Another middle school teacher (Clara) calls by Jenny's office. She is obviously excited about something. 'I've just been talking to Maria in my class, Jenny, and I've realised what the problem is!' Jenny invites her in to hear more. Maria is the non-English speaking student that Clara has chosen to interview as part of the inquiry. 'Maria told me about how much she could do at her school in Mexico. She showed me some of the maths she had been doing. She must be bored silly by where our class is at—she's way past all that, but I hadn't noticed.' In the next fortnight, several teachers pop in to share insights with Jenny. Talking with the students is exploding some myths and raising some new questions.

Beginning to focus

The staff get together again in Week 3, and this time there seems to be more energy around the idea of a collaborative inquiry. Curiosity about learners and their experiences is starting to come to the fore. The teachers (mostly) are eager to share what their students said, and Jenny has collated the comments into a document for all the teachers to work on in groups. A consensus seems to be emerging that maybe mathematics would be a good focus for the inquiry: no-one looked at it in Term 1, so everyone is starting from the same place, and the NAPLAN and PAT-M results are very low.

In addition, a lot of interesting information about mathematics has been shared by the students in their interviews, particularly when comparing it with comments about reading. The higher achieving students seem to be asking for harder mathematics and less repetition. The others needed to change their understanding of mathematics as more than learning basic facts and getting the right answer.

Jenny realises that the focus on 'mathematics' is too broad but doesn't want to quell the teachers' enthusiasm. She realises that the first three phases of the spiral go back and forth as teachers learn more about what is happening for learners and start to examine their hunches. Through this process a more manageable focus is likely to emerge.

Developing a hunch

Jenny decides that the difficult, and sometimes challenging, nature of developing hunches is best done by working together on a student-free day because this creates space for the teachers to work together and really nut out how they might be contributing to the students' mathematics achievement.

Despite Jenny setting the scene by describing that hunches focus on how the teachers and leaders are contributing to the current situation, the teachers' initial hunches were all about the assessments, the students and their parents. Some examples include:

- NAPLAN and PAT-M are not good measures of what we value and teach in mathematics.
- Parents have old-fashioned expectations and part of the problem is them teaching their children the wrong ways at home.
- We can't use equipment at maths time because the children can't be trusted not to throw it or nick it.
- Refugee and Aboriginal and Torres Strait Islander children are so poor at focusing that we need to break things down into really small chunks so they can get a bit at a time—they need structure and predictability and lots of rote practice.

One of the team leaders, who is still not happy about working together as a school and was beginning to feel that people were saying her teaching wasn't good enough, adds: 'It's not realistic to expect these students to achieve at the same level as kids at other schools. They are coming from poor backgrounds, with uninvolved families and no support—they are not going to go on to professional roles so making their lives miserable with too much maths is counterproductive. They don't like maths and making them do it won't help.'

Jenny draws the discussion back to the student interview data, particularly the two themes of contrasting answers given by the lower achieving students about their learning in reading and mathematics, and the comments by the higher achieving students about mathematics being boring and repetitive. The nods she notices across the room embolden her to put forward the challenge, 'Maybe it is the way we teach maths that is creating some of the problems'.

After a break, Clara adds: 'I've been looking again at the data and I'm wondering if we are focusing on the wrong thing. Sure, achievement is low, but it seems to me that year-on-year, progress is slow. Maybe we think the students can't achieve highly, but surely they can make more progress than they are at moment if we do things differently.'

This comment gives the staff a new direction to think about—and new hunches form:

- We don't really know what progress looks like on some of the big stuff—what should they be able to do? We are much more confident about progress on the 'mechanics' of mathematics.
- We know about the curriculum but it's too broad, it's the smaller steps we don't know.

One teacher, John, a mathematics curriculum leader who has just completed a Master's paper in teaching mathematics, has been silent up to now. At Jenny's invitation, he comments: 'There seem to be a couple of things that are holding students back, even our 'top' students, but it's even more of a problem for our struggling students. They don't seem to understand how numbers work and that makes understanding other things difficult.' Clara asks, 'How do you even teach that? How numbers work? I can see why it's an issue, I just don't know where to start to teach it'.

A sharper focus

Clara's willingness to state her vulnerability changes the atmosphere in the staffroom. Under John's guidance, with Jenny's support, over the next few weeks, the staff coalesce around the idea of looking at 'how numbers work', through the key concept of place value. It is clear from the student achievement evidence that this is an issue, and it is clear from the teachers' hunches that they are not sure how to address it. Learning and teaching place value becomes Hilly Primary School's focus. It is manageable for teachers and likely to make a big difference for students, particularly those whose understanding of mathematics is limited to basic facts and the right answers. Jenny outlines the work the school is doing in a newsletter to parents.

Professional learning

Jenny invites a local mathematics facilitator to come in for three staff meeting sessions and work with John and the staff to increase their pedagogical content knowledge of place value. They develop a continuum of progress on place value through the year levels and use a common task with increasing complexity across year levels to place their target students on a data wall. This brings to life 'what progress looks like', where each student is at and what they need to know next. Once they know this, they realise it is much easier to work out how to teach it. One of the many surprises is that some of these target students know a lot more about place value than the teachers thought, while the knowledge of others is shakier.

Taking action

The teachers agree to run a three-week focused unit on place value across the school, and to share their ideas from the beginning of Term 3. The team leaders and John work hard with the mathematics facilitator to provide the teachers with resources and materials. Discussions about place value, the best ways to teach it, models that could be used and the likely pathways for children spill over into the staffroom during breaks.

In the holidays before Term 3 begins, Jenny gets a call from the State Education Office. A new initiative on children's writing is being rolled out by the State and Hilly Primary is on the list for Term 3. A facilitator will come to work with staff at five staff meetings and will observe the teachers in their classrooms and provide feedback. This is a generous offer, and writing is certainly an issue, but participating in the initiative would derail the mathematics-focused inquiry. Jenny wonders about whether she should try and get the staff to do both or take up the writing offer instead of persisting with mathematics. It is tempting to buy in to something with so much structure and support—leading the mathematics inquiry is tiring and confusing because they have to work so much out for themselves. In the end, though, she decides to stick with the progress she has made and asks if Hilly Primary can join in next year.

Checking

Jenny is pleased she turned down the writing initiative when she walks through the school in the first three weeks of term. There is a real buzz among the staff and the students about the place value focus. Although the teachers agreed to wait until the end of the unit before moving students on the data wall, most of the teachers can't restrain themselves as they notice some students moving from one level to the next. Shifting students on the data wall becomes a daily occurrence that Jenny makes a point of celebrating. One of the teachers is even seen doing a 'happy dance' in the staffroom to celebrate a breakthrough for one of her most challenging learners. Jenny comments on this positive focus and feeling in the room.

At the end of the three-week unit, the teachers repeat the common task with their target students. When they meet together to discuss the results it is clear that there have been large gains for all but nine students. While everyone is pleased at the improvement, and feels empowered by their ability to develop the students' place value concepts, Jenny is most pleased to hear one of the teachers say, 'But what about these nine students? Why didn't it work for them?' They are moving into a deeper spiral of inquiry without realising it.

The buzz has also reached parents, who are starting to ask about what is happening. Jenny is amazed at how much enthusiasm and curiosity has been generated through the inquiry process.

MOUNTAINS COLLEGE

Starting with the solution

Mountains College is a Year 7–12 public school situated on the boundary of two suburbs, both middle to high socio-economic communities. A total of 23 per cent of the 1535 students have language backgrounds other than English, 5 per cent identify as having Aboriginal or Torres Strait Islander heritage, and 10 per cent are funded under the Program for Students with a Disability.

The College is led by a principal and three associate principals. Of the associate principals, one is responsible for teaching and learning; one is responsible for curriculum and pathways; and one is responsible for pastoral care, community connection and the learning environment. This senior leadership team is supplemented by six leading teachers who have some class release to work on cross-school projects and the heads of faculty for each learning area, who also receive some release time to lead their subject areas.

For the last two years, Mountains College has been looking at assessment to make it more meaningful to students and in line with the intent of the Australian curriculum. They had outside experts take sessions with staff, focusing on designing engaging and authentic assessment tasks that link to students' lives and experiences.

In recent years, the style of external assessment for the senior students has changed too, with an increase in written answers and explanations in subjects that have traditionally been assessed by short-answer or multi-choice questions. Even in mathematics, students are having to provide explanations for their working and discuss how their answer fits in to the scenario posed in the question. These trends mean that the students need to be clear, accurate and fluent in their written work.

Teachers have become concerned that the students don't seem to be able to put their ideas into paragraphs that clearly demonstrate their knowledge and are getting lower marks than they should. In addition, previously high-achieving students are objecting to the new assessment approach because they are not doing as well as they used to.

The leadership team met at the end of the previous year to brainstorm a focus for professional learning for this current year. The leading teachers, and the head of English, reported on 'rumbling' from staff, students and parents about the changes to assessment. Everyone seemed concerned that the students cannot show what they know adequately and there was some pushback from some of the students about the new assessment approach. The team decided to suggest to the staff that literacy across the curriculum be their new focus for professional learning.

The presentation of this the idea to staff at a student-free day got a mixed reception. Some staff felt they should have been consulted about the focus and wanted input. They thought that jumping into literacy across the curriculum was a knee-jerk reaction. Others in the PE and mathematics faculties felt that the focus wasn't very relevant for them and wanted to be able to spend their share of the professional learning resource on something more valuable to their subject areas. At the end of the day the senior leadership team agreed to go 'back to the drawing board' and think again about their approach.

After thinking about the teachers' reactions, the leadership team decided to start again. They realised they had jumped to a solution without knowing what was happening for all their learners and what the issues really were.

Scanning

They decided to use the spiral of inquiry as the guiding framework for their new approach. The spiral of inquiry would open up opportunities for all the teachers to inquire into what was happening for their learners and to use this to identify a focus that directly addressed the students' needs in the specific curriculum areas and would allow the teachers to contribute their expertise. They also heard the message that maybe they were acting on a few anecdotal stories or complaints and overreacting. Was literacy in assessment really an issue for the students? The spiral of inquiry's focus on the use of evidence gave the leadership team a new starting point to work with their staff.

In February, the leadership team called a series of whole-staff meetings. The meetings were an hour long and a week apart, so there was time for teachers to think in between, but not so long that they lost momentum. At the first meeting they began with an overview of the spiral of inquiry with a particular focus on scanning and posed the question, 'What do you think is the biggest learning challenge for our students?' Many different ideas flowed from this question. Given the importance of evidence in the spiral, the leadership team agreed to update and collate all the information that they had used to identify the issue with literacy for the next staff meeting. This evidence included data from internal assessments, performance on final year qualifications, NAPLAN Year 7 and 9 for the last three years, and an engagement and school climate survey.

All teachers agreed to interview three students over the following week who were struggling with the new assessment. They were to ask them three questions:

'Where are you going with your learning—do you have learning goals for this subject?', 'Did the information you got from last year's assessment tell you how you were going?' and 'Did this information tell you what you needed to learn next?'

At the next week's meeting, staff were put into mixed curriculum groups to discuss the interview data and the evidence provided by the leadership team. Students' responses to the three questions showed some consistent patterns. Few had clear learning goals beyond 'passing'. When teachers gave a mark, they thought that told them how they were going but probing of these answers identified that the students thought passing depended on how intelligent they were. They didn't see assessment as helping them to identify what they needed to learn next because end-of-unit assessments were focused on what they had completed, not what was coming next.

In the third meeting, the associate principal in charge of teaching and learning led a discussion about themes that emerged from all the information the teachers had engaged with. The staff named several themes:

- Students in our school view assessment as separate from learning with marks reflecting their ability rather than their effort.
- Students prefer, and did well on, short-answer/multiple-choice questions because they know how to study for them and answer them.
- There is slower than expected growth between Years 7 and 9, but the students seem to do as well as expected on the State levels in the senior school exams.
- Our students seem to be good with facts and mastering knowledge, but they are not so good at interpreting, inferring and problem solving.
- Students feel good about coming to school and feel it is safe.

This summary sparked a lot of curiosity among the staff. Why weren't the students able to apply what they knew to new questions or more real-life scenarios? Was this a learning problem, an attitude problem or an assessment problem? These questions also raised angst among some staff who felt the leadership team were criticising them.

Focusing

The six leading teachers, and three others who were interested, formed into a professional learning team (PLT), led by the associate principal in charge of teaching and learning. They undertook to work on the staff's ideas and come back with a proposed focus that would be the school's inquiry for the year. After discussion they decided that, while they knew what the teachers thought and they had some scanning data from some students about their perception that assessment was disconnected from learning, they didn't have enough student voice to be able to answer the questions about learning, attitude or assessment.

The PLT undertook to speak to five students each from their classes during the coming week to probe these issues and to bring their comments back to the next PLT meeting.

The next meeting of the PLT was exciting: the discussions with the students had brought forward some really interesting ideas and given the team new perspectives on the focus area. The students' responses differed a bit by year level but, in general, they expressed frustration at not being asked the 'right' questions for what they had been taught. A Year 11 student said: 'We practise loads of examples in class and get really good at them, and then in the test it's always put the other way around, or in a word problem or something, and you just can't recognise it.' A Year 10 student, for whom English is a second language, explained: 'I know all the terms and diagrams, but then we have to read three sources in the exam and evaluate them and I can't read them fast enough. If they just asked me to list and define the key ideas, I could do that.' The students seemed to value their ability to 'know' or 'remember' over their ability to use their knowledge and resented the added burden of applying their knowledge that often appeared in assessment tasks. 'I used to be able to get really good marks. I just don't see the purpose of the new way of doing it. It's like they try and make it 'real' to be interesting, but it's not real, it's school and it should look like school', said a Year 12 student. These kinds of comments helped the team to realise that the issue encompassed all of the issues about what it means to learn something and to have it assessed.

The real-life application scenarios that the teachers worked hard to create seemed to be missing the mark. There was a much deeper problem. The PLT also realised that, while they had looked at year-level differences, they had not considered whether gender and diversity of learner background affected the achievement levels nor if the students were more successful in some subjects than others. They needed to check what evidence was missing and see what other messages might be in the evidence they had.

The PLT went back to the whole-staff group suggesting that they deliberately analyse which groups of students were impacted by the new assessment practice with four possible related foci to improving things:

- engaging students in a deeper understanding of what it means to learn something
- addressing the 'ability' versus 'effort' perception
- improving students' engagement with, and responses to, tasks that required them to apply their knowledge in new situations

- helping the students to see the links between assessment and learning.

The PLT shared some of the students' contributions with the staff and reminded them of the data they had looked at, this time with subgroups disaggregated. The suggested four focus areas created a buzz in the meeting as teachers from different faculties talked about what it would mean for their subject areas. The nature of the focus could be applied across all curriculum areas and it aligned with the overall direction of the curriculum. Some teachers, however, had little to say.

There was also discussion about the students who the teachers perceived 'never bothered engaging' anyway. One teacher said that Aboriginal and Torres Strait Islander students would be disadvantaged because they were already failing and this would make it harder for them to access learning. When the associate principal put up the data by ethnicity again to check this out, the staff could see that Aboriginal and Torres Strait Islander students were not all in the lower achievement groups and that, while cultural needs should be explored and catered for, this generalisation was not borne out in the data.

There was some discussion about whether new English language learners could cope with this way of learning. One of the leadership team was completing her Master's degree and said recent research had shown that teaching in this way benefitted these students, many of whom were highly sophisticated conceptually in their own language, but were being 'taught down to' in many classrooms.

Teachers expressed concern that the new methods of assessment were disadvantaging boys. They argued that girls were better at writing than boys. Teachers were surprised to see that boys' data had not significantly worsened relative to girls' results with the new assessments. The gender gap remained the same.

Developing a hunch

The next step in the spiral of inquiry involves developing hunches, and the leadership team decided to ask the staff to do this task in faculty groups and report back at a student-free day at the end of the first term. Hunches are about understanding how the adults may be contributing to the students' current understanding of learning and assessment. A couple of teachers appeared somewhat anxious about exploring the idea that they as adults might be contributing to a student's problematic understanding of assessment. One of the associate principals noticed this and mentioned to everyone that this is important work that can sometimes feel uncomfortable but that is a normal part of the process.

As with most groups first working on hunches, they started with a focus on the students not the teachers. For example, the science team came up with an initial list of hunches:
- Students don't complete homework tasks where often the 'extras' are covered.
- Students aren't listening in class and don't pick up the main ideas well.
- Students don't use the textbook properly.
- Boys don't like writing.

The PLT members met to discuss this issue and agreed they needed to shift the teachers back to how they were contributing. Some staff were uncomfortable about doing this and the principal acknowledged this can make you feel a bit vulnerable as an educator but is an important part of being an effective educator. Eventually different lists emerged that included hunches like:
- We prefer to teach facts and details rather than conceptual frameworks and application because this is what the students expect, and it leads to fewer behaviour problems. This has led to some misalignment of our teaching and the new assessments.
- We introduced the new assessments without much explanation or discussion about learning and applying knowledge with either parents or students.
- Our continuing to use marks, rather than feedback and explanations, has led to students not connecting assessment and learning.
- We possibly underestimate the abilities of new learners of English and maybe teach Aboriginal and Torres Strait Islander students in ways that lead them to see little meaning in their learning.
- Maybe we have different expectations for boys and written assessments.

Following from this, a biology teacher, Sara, noted:

> *I think what we were hearing from the students, though, and what I see in my class data, is that they think the task is to rote learn. How are they getting that message? When I look at what I've done this term I can see that, although in my head we are learning key principles, the students might not see that. We do a lot of exercises and I have PowerPoints of vocab to help the English language learners that I use a lot. I'm not sure if I'm coming over to the students as I mean to. Then I give a mark.*

They realised that their new focus needed to include changing and aligning teaching and assessment together with helping students to understand what it means to learn something deeply and how effort is a better predictor of success than ability.

Some teachers clearly felt uncomfortable about this focus because it meant changing how they thought about teaching and what it meant to be successful.

Although no-one expressed this directly, the leadership team recognised that some staff would need a great deal of support to change. They realised they would need to make it manageable, so asked faculties if they were prepared to take this approach with their Year 7s and 8s for two units over one term. Most enthusiasm was expressed by staff in science, humanities and social sciences (HSS), and health and physical education (HPE), as long as they had support.

Learning

The leadership team organised professional learning opportunities for all the staff involved together and in their separate faculties. They were given additional release time to plan together. This appeared to be going well until one of the PE teachers proposed enrolling in an advanced sports coaching programme that they felt was more relevant to their roles. The principal felt strongly that part of the power of the inquiry spiral was the shared focus and insisted that the PE teachers honour their commitment and continue to participate in the inquiry, promising them they could enrol in the sports coaching program next year with her support. Attendance by HPE teachers at the professional learning sessions dropped off as Term 2 proceeded.

The learning phase of the inquiry spiral took all of Term 2. Some teachers started to change their practice at the same time as doing the professional learning, while others bided their time and continued as usual.

Taking action

The HSS teachers decided to try introducing their new unit on World War I with Year 8 with a series of letters sent by a soldier from the front, rather than with a chronological overview and timeline as they had before. The students would be invited to explore the letters and draw conclusions from them, without first learning any 'facts' about World War I. The teachers hoped that engaging with primary sources and working 'like historians' with the material, before learning about key events and their consequences, would increase the students' ability to understand World War I holistically.

The faculty head (Mike) didn't have a Year 8 class, so he decided to visit the teachers as they taught the initial lessons they had planned together. In one room, Mike watched as the teacher (Natasha) showed a YouTube clip summary of World War I origins. The students had a blank timeline, and Natasha paused the video at key moments and prompted the students to record the events on their timelines. At the end of the lesson Natasha asked the students to use their textbooks to extend the timeline to the end of 1914 and to complete this for homework. Mike was surprised, as he had expected to see the 'letters lesson' that they had collaboratively planned. Why hadn't Natasha tried the new lesson? Mike thought maybe in his role as faculty head he needed to support Natasha further to understand the change process and find out what she needed in order to feel safe in trying something new.

Checking

They also decided on student interviews and surveys at the end of the term to see if their understanding of, and attitudes to, learning and assessment were changing. Even though the students were supposedly being exposed to the same ideas in science, HSS and HPE, it was clear that they compartmentalised their understanding and attitudes according to the subject. Interviews showed big shifts were evident in science, some shifts in social science but none in HPE where, in essence, nothing had changed.

The students reported positive responses to teachers starting units or lessons with 'big problems or ideas' in science and to some extent in HSS. They particularly liked having the application tasks at the beginning so they could see where they were heading, rather than at the end where they felt like a nasty surprise. They were better able to put their ideas into paragraphs that demonstrated their knowledge and their marks were improving. The students felt that the assessments were now more aligned with the work they had done in class than they were before.

The leadership team asked the PLT to come together again to think about where the school was at in the inquiry spiral and to recommend what to do next. All the science department and most of the HSS teachers wanted to continue to teach in this way. The issue for the leadership team and the PLT was to spread the more effective teaching, learning and assessment practices so these became the learning culture across the whole school, where students understood what they were learning and why, were able to apply their learning and write about it and engage with the understanding that their effort was what counted most.

Re-scanning

Over Term 4, the PLT engaged closely with staff and students who had been involved in the spiral, both those who had made the change and those who had not. They sought to understand what facilitated change and what had got in the way so they could use that information to create the change across the whole school.

Towards the end of the year, a group of students approached the PLT leader and talked about how the new approach had made so much difference to them in terms of both their learning and how they felt about themselves as learners. They agreed to come to the final staff meeting of the year and repeat what they had said and answer questions. The more sceptical teachers questioned the students closely and were clearly thinking about what it could mean for the teachers. This presentation proved to be the catalyst for the beginning of a whole school change. All faculties agreed to 'have a go' although it was still clear some teachers were not convinced. Faculty heads were asked to inquire about the issues for those teachers so they could put in the right support in the new year. This would probably involve some challenging of established ways of doing things as well.

CHAPTER 7
Bringing things together for impact

This book is about practical strategies for leaders to realise the potential for professional learning and development in their schools as part of their improvement processes. While it may feel like another expectation for school leaders to do this work, it has become central to the role of school leadership teams as awareness grows that development activities located outside of schools typically have little impact on what happens in schools. Context matters.

Context matters because improvement in any aspect of leading, teaching and learning interacts with, and impacts on, other aspects so needs to be led holistically. This means considering current beliefs, vulnerabilities, knowledge and the wider school culture. These things are not background to learning and change, they are part of it. Removing one 'bit' of professional practice, trying to change it, then reinserting it back into the complexity of existing contexts typically does not work. Yet we often act as if it should. Teachers enrol in 'courses' to learn new ways to teach something with the implication that existing practice could be improved. Yet they are seldom asked if they believe there to be a problem or if they want to change what they already do. Leaders go to conferences to keep up to date, but such attendance rarely impacts deeply on their ability to create coherence, develop a learning culture or use evidence more effectively.

We have written separate chapters in this book on coherence; developing a learning culture; emotion and vulnerability in the change process; using evidence and evaluative thinking; and finally, issues of equity, bias and beliefs. These challenges, however, cannot be separated from one another; they are interrelated. It is more a matter of what is foreground and what is background rather than putting boundaries on each one. For example, starting the inquiry process with evidence of student learning can create feelings of anxiety and vulnerability for teachers, particularly if a strong learning culture has not been established and teachers are worried about being blamed for variable student outcomes. These feelings disappear when curiosity takes over, together with a commitment to making a difference to student learning. But these emotions might arise again when issues of equity and bias become evident when the evidence shows that some students are benefitting more from the change process than others. Coherence is difficult to maintain if there are competing priorities and the inquiry process has not demonstrated the shift in student outcomes all hope for. Doing something new or different is easier than inquiring more deeply.

When these attributes come together through an inquiry process, meaningful change occurs. Everyone's motivation improves, anxiety and vulnerability disappear as a learning culture becomes part of 'how we do things around here'. Evidence about what is going on for learners is sought in every phase with teachers unwilling to move to the next idea until they have understood things sufficiently deeply to make a difference and had a chance to embed new practices. We have illustrated how these challenges interweave through our description of the two cases in Chapter 6.

Enthusiasm and commitment for the change and improvement agenda arise from better and sustained outcomes for learners. This happens when leaders recognise that professional learning and improvement is a complex process, rather than a linear one. In the Preface to this book we described the challenges of teaching in terms of meeting the needs of diverse learners in complex settings interacting in unpredictable ways with an uncertain curriculum (Le Fevre et al., 2015). It is meaningless to try to separate the learners from the learning environments and what they are supposed to learn. Leaders have another layer of complexity to take into account as they promote the professional learning of diverse teacher learners who interact in unpredictable ways with their professional learning context, the student learners they teach and the curriculum they are required to teach them. None of this learning and improvement happens in isolation or in a straight line.

The work of Heifetz, Grashow, and Linsky (2009) from Harvard Business School is relevant here. They differentiated technical problems from adaptive challenges in business. The same applies in schools. Technical problems are relatively easy to identify, can be solved with new information or a new skillset because they have known solutions that can be taught. Solving them is best supported by a teacher–learner relationship where the 'teacher' may be a leader or a professional developer. Unfortunately, few of these kinds of problems arise in the life of schools. Adaptive challenges, on the other hand, have no predictable known solutions and they are as easy to deny or resist as to acknowledge them. Heifetz et al. (2009) found that sustainable solutions to these types of challenges usually require changes in how we think and act. They propose that adaptive challenges need to be navigated through in every phase, a process that is best supported by collaborative inquiry.

There are many inquiry processes described in the literature and all have merit. We have used the spiral of inquiry as the framing of our approach because it is consistent with the evidence on professional learning with high impact (Timperley et al., 2007) by starting with investigating the experiences of learners. The spiral emphasises collaboration and developing teachers' agency. It is very much about navigating solutions and seeking evidence to check impact. Table 7.1 provides an overview of the kind of shifts involved in inquiry processes that address adaptive challenges.

Thinking about these shifts can highlight where you are doing well and where you may want to direct your future efforts. Although school improvement work is difficult and can seem never-ending, it can make a real difference for students, their families and those who teach them. When students are at the centre, it is all worth it. One deputy principal with whom we worked explains what happened at her school, as she thought about before and after the staff used the spiral of inquiry to improve their students' mathematics learning:

> *I think the most obvious change would be the idea of having professional learning teams, the collaboration with staff, the dialogue with staff, the use of evidence, I think. None of those things [was] particularly evident before we started using the spiral of inquiry and now it's what you would see everywhere. You would see data walls in each of the staff offices. You would see staff working together. We have team planning time now. We didn't have team planning time before, but now teams are all released during the day to have their planning together, so there [are] so many things you would see now than you may not have seen back then.*

> *In terms of student learning, I think there [were] probably a lot of just worksheets that were probably given before we did the spiral. There was lots of teacher talk that was used. So it was probably teacher talk and worksheets beforehand but now you would see explicit teaching, you would see small focus groups, you would see lots of hands-on, you would see lots of different things going on, not just relying on the students listening for their information. I guess all of the work that's been done has changed the practice in the classroom, so the students are the ones that then get the better lessons, they get teachers who are more inspired,*

> *teachers who know what they are doing, teachers who are interested in what the students have to say about their learning and how they like to learn.*
>
> *Deputy Principal, K–8 school*

TABLE 7.1: Overview of shifts in an inquiry process

From …	To …
Seeing education challenges as complicated, able to be pulled apart and dealt with using specific interventions on the pieces	Seeing education challenges as complex, made up of fundamentally interdependent parts and needing to be considered as wholes
Working to incrementally improve the status quo	Working to transform the status quo, understanding how practices at all levels can reproduce inequity
Acting on the basis of one's experience alone	Recognising that one's experience is shaped by cultural positioning and framed by one's worldview, and that others might be different
Using prepared programs or materials in the same way across contexts	Choosing from a range of resources to respond to the needs of a particular context
Acting on a hunch	Acting on a broad range of evidence and investigating hunches to explain it
Being the expert who knows what to do	Being a co-learner who has an open mind
Approaching change with tools	Approaching change with questions
Doing what you know you do well in the way you always do it	Inquiring into the experience of the people you are working with and monitoring the impact of your actions
Doing what you planned	Doing what they need and adjusting according to the evidence
Beginning with the teachers	Beginning with the learners, especially those marginalised by our education systems

Professional learning and schooling improvement are complex. Bearing this in mind, exercising agency and doing what you can to help teachers learn how they can help students learn can put the whole school on a learning trajectory and create a learning culture. Leaders of professional learning and leaders of schools have power: this book is about using it to improve all learners' learning, achievement and wellbeing.

References

Ainscow, M. (2016). Collaboration as a strategy for promoting equity in education: Possibilities and barriers. *Journal of Professional Capital and Community*, 1(2), 159–172. doi:10.1108/JPCC-12-2015-0013

Australian Council for Educational Research (ACER). (2018). *Principal Performance Improvement Tool*. Camberwell, VIC: Author. Retrieved from https://research.acer.edu.au/cgi/viewcontent.cgi?article=1032&context=tll_misc

Australian Council for Educational Research, & the Queensland Department of Education, Training and Employment. (2012). *National School Improvement Tool*. Camberwell, VIC: Author. Retrieved from www.acer.edu.au/nsit

Australian Human Rights Commission. (2014). Face the Facts: Cultural Diversity. Sydney, NSW: Author. Retrieved from https://www.humanrights.gov.au/our-work/education/face-facts-cultural-diversity

Australian Institute for Teaching and School Leadership (AITSL). (2011). *Australian Professional Standards for Teachers*. Melbourne, VIC: Author. Retrieved from https://www.aitsl.edu.au/docs/default-source/national-policy-framework/australian-professional-standards-for-teachers.pdf?sfvrsn=5800f33c_64

Australian Institute for Teaching and School Leadership (AITSL). (2015). *Australian Professional Standard for Principals and the Leadership Profiles* (pp. 1–32) [ebook]. Melbourne, VIC: Author. Retrieved from www.aitsl.edu.au/docs/default-source/default-document-library/australian-professional-standard-for-principals-and-the-leadership-profiles652c8891b1e86477b58fff00006709da.pdf?sfvrsn=11c4ec3c_0

Barth, R. S. (2002). The culture builder. *Educational Leadership*, 59(8), 6–11.

Bishop, R. (2010). Effective teaching for indigenous and minoritized students. *Procedia Social and Behavioural Sciences*, 7, 57–62.

Blank, A., Hokomau, C., & Kingi, H. (2016). *Unconscious bias and education: A comparative study of Maori and African American students* [Report]. Auckland, NZ: Oranui Diversity Leadership. Retrieved from http://oranui.co.nz/images/oranui_reports/unconscious-bias-and-education.pdf

Bryk, A., Sebring, P. Allensworth, E., Luppescu, S., & Easton, J. (2010). *Organizing schools for improvement*. Chicago, IL: University of Chicago Press.

Cochran-Smith, M., Ell, F., Ludlow, L., Grudnoff, L., & Aitken, G. (2014). The challenge and promise of complexity theory for teacher education research. *Teachers College Record*, 116(5), 1–38.

DuFour, R. (2011). Work together: But only if you want to. *The Phi Delta Kappan*, 92(5), 57–61.

Dumont, H., Istance, D., & Benavides, F. (Eds.). (2010). *The nature of learning: Using research to inspire practice*. Paris: OECD.

Earl, L., & Katz, S. (2010). Creating a culture of inquiry: Harnessing data for professional learning. In A. Blankstein, P. Houston, & R. Cole (Eds.), *Data enhanced leadership series: The soul of educational leadership*. Thousand Oaks, CA: Corwin Press.

Earl, L., & Timperley, H. (2015). Evaluative thinking for successful educational innovation. *OECD Working Papers*, No. 122. Paris: OECD Publishing. Retrieved from https://doi.org/10.1787/5jrxtk1jtdwf-en

Earl, L., & Timperley, H. S. (2016). *Embedding evaluative thinking as an essential component of successful innovation*. Seminar paper 257. Melbourne, VIC: Centre for Strategic Education.

Edmondson, A. C. (1999). Psychological safety and learning behaviour in work teams. *Administrative Science Quarterly*, 44, 350–383. doi:10.2307/2666999

Forrest, J., Lean, G., & Dunn, K. (2016). Challenging racism through schools: Teacher attitudes to cultural diversity and multicultural education in Sydney, Australia. *Race Ethnicity and Education*, 19(3), 618–638. doi:10.1080/13613324.2015.1095170

Francis, B., Mills, M., & Lupton, R. (2017). Towards social justice in education: Contradictions and dilemmas. *Journal of Education Policy*, 32(4), 414–431. doi:10.1080/02680939.2016.1276218

Fullan, M., & Hargreaves, A. (1996). *What's worth fighting for in your school?* New York: Teachers College Press.

Gorringe, S. (2015, May 15). Aboriginal culture is not a problem. The way we talk about it is. *The Guardian*. Retrieved from www.theguardian.com/commentisfree/2015/may/15/aboriginal-culture-is-not-a-problem-the-way-we-talk-about-it-is

Hattie, J. (2015). *What works best in education: The politics of collaborative expertise*. London: Pearson. Retrieved from www.pearson.com/content/dam/corporate/global/pearson-dot-com/files/hattie/150526_ExpertiseWEB_V1.pdf

Heifetz, R. A., Grashow, A., & Linsky., M. (2009). *The practice of adaptive leadership: Tools and tactics for changing your organization and the word*. Boston, MA: Harvard Business School.

Hynds, A., Averill, R., Penetito, W., Meyer, L., Hindle R., & Faircloth, S. (2016). Examining the impediments to Indigenous strategy and approaches in mainstream secondary schools. *International Journal of Leadership in Education, 19*(5), 534–556. doi:10.1080/13603124.2015.1051130

Ishimaru, A., & Galloway, M. K. (2014). Beyond individual effectiveness: Conceptualizing organizational leadership for equity. *Leadership and Policy in Schools, 13*(1), 93–146. doi:10.1080/15700763.2014.890733

James, M. (2006). Assessment, teaching and theories of learning. In J. Gardner (Ed.), *Assessment and learning* (pp. 47–60). London: Sage.

Jensen, B., Sonnemann, J., Roberts-Hull, K., & Hunter, A. (2016). *Beyond PD: Teacher professional learning in high-performing systems* (Australian ed.) Washington, DC: National Center on Education and the Economy.

Kahneman, D. (2011). *Thinking, fast and slow*. London, England: Penguin Books.

Katz, S., & Dack, L. (2013). *Intentional interruption: Breaking down learning barriers to transform professional practice*. Thousand Oaks, CA: Corwin Press.

Katz, S., Earl, L., & Ben Jaafar, S. (2009). *Building and connecting learning communities: The power of networks for school improvement*. Thousand Oaks, CA: Corwin Press.

Kenway, J. (2013). Challenging inequality in Australian schools: Gonski and beyond. *Discourse: Studies in the Cultural Politics of Education, 34*(2), 286–308, doi:10.1080/01596306.2013.770254

Le Fevre, D. M., Robinson, V. M. J., & Sinnema, C. E. L. (2015). Genuine inquiry: Widely espoused but rarely enacted. *Educational Management Administration and Leadership, 43*(6), 883–899.

Le Fevre, D. M., Timperley, H., & Ell, F. (2015). Curriculum and pedagogy: The future of teacher professional learning and the development of adaptive expertise. In D. Wyse, L. Hayward, & J. Pandya (Eds.), *The SAGE handbook of curriculum, pedagogy, and assessment* (pp. 309–324). Thousand Oaks, CA: Sage.

McDonald, J. P. (1992). *Teaching: Making sense of an uncertain craft*. New York: Teachers College Press.

McKenzie, K. B., & Phillips, G. A. (2016). Equity traps then and now: Deficit thinking, racial erasure and naïve acceptance of meritocracy. *Whiteness and Education, 1*(1), 26–38. doi10.1080/23793406.2016.115960

Meissel, K., Meyer, F., Yao, E., & Rubie-Davies, C. (2017). Subjectivity of teacher judgments: Exploring student characteristics that influence teacher judgments of student ability. *Teaching and Teacher Education, 65*, 48–60.

MET Project. (2013). *Ensuring fair and reliable measures of effective teaching: Culminating findings from the MET project's three-year study*. Seattle, WA: The Bill and Melinda Gates Foundation. Retrieved from http://k12education.

gatesfoundation.org/download/?Num=2572&filename=MET_Ensuring_Fair_and_Reliable_Measures_Practitioner_Brief.pdf

OECD. (2012). *Equity and quality in education: Supporting disadvantaged students and schools.* Paris: OECD Publishing. Retrieved from http://dx.doi.org/10.1787/9789264130852-en

Opfer, V. D., & Pedder, D. (2011). Conceptualizing teacher professional learning. *Review of Educational Research, 81*(3), 376–407.

Pellegrino, J., & Hilton, M. (2012). *Education for life and work: Developing transferrable knowledge and skills in the 21st century.* Washington, DC: National Research Council.

Robinson, V., Bendikson, L., McNaughton, S., Wilson, A., & Zhu, T. (2017). Joining the dots: The challenge of creating coherent school improvement. *Teachers College Record, 119,* 1–44.

Robinson, V., Lloyd, C., & Hohepa, M. (2009). *School leadership and student outcomes: Identifying what works and why: Best evidence synthesis iteration.* Wellington, NZ: Ministry of Education.

Robinson, V., McNaughton, S., & Timperley, H. (2011). Building capacity in a self-managing schooling system: The New Zealand experience. *Journal of Education Administration, 49*(6), 720–728.

Sarra, C., Spillman, D., Jackson, C., Davis, J., & Bray, J. (2018). High-expectations relationships: A foundation for enacting high expectations in all Australian schools. *The Australian Journal of Indigenous Education,* 1–14. doi:10.1017/jie.2018.10

Schein, E. H. (2017). *Organizational culture and leadership* (5th ed.). Hoboken, NJ: John Wiley.

Sleeter, C. E. (2008). Preparing white teachers for diverse students. In M. Cochran-Smith, S. Feiman-Nemser, & J. McIntyre (Eds.), *Handbook of research in teacher education: Enduring issues in changing contexts* (3rd ed., pp. 559–582). New York: Routledge.

Stone, D., Patton, B., & Heen, S. (2010). Difficult conversations: How to discuss what matters most. New York: Penguin.

Stronger Smarter Institute. (2014). *High-expectations relationships: A foundation for quality learning environments in all Australian schools.* Position paper. Brisbane, QLD: Author.

Thomson, S., De Bortoli, S., & Underwood, C. (2016). *PISA 2015: A first look at Australia's results.* Camberwell, VIC: ACER.

Timperley, H. (2011). *Realizing the power of professional learning.* London: Open University Press.

Timperley, H. (2014). Developing teacher effectiveness through professional conversations. In O. Tan (Ed.), *International perspectives on policy and practice for building new teacher competencies* (pp. 189–208). Singapore: Cengage Publishing.

Timperley, H., Kaser, L., & Halbert, J. (2014). *A framework for transforming learning in schools: Innovation and the spiral of inquiry.* Seminar paper 234. Melbourne, VIC: Centre for Strategic Education.

Timperley, H., & Parr, J. (2009). Chain of influence from policy to practice in the New Zealand literacy strategy. *Research Papers in Education, 24*(2), 135–154.

Timperley, H. S., & Robinson, V. M. J. (2001). Achieving school improvement through challenging and changing teachers' schema. *Journal of Educational Change, 2,* 281–300.

Timperley, H., Wilson, A., Barrar, H., & Fung, I. (2007). *Teacher professional learning and development: Best evidence synthesis iteration* (BES). Wellington, NZ: Ministry of Education.

Timperley, H., Wilson, A., Barrar, H., & Fung, I. (2008). *Best evidence synthesis on professional learning and development* (Report to the Ministry of Education). Wellington, NZ: Ministry of Education.

Twyford, K., & Le Fevre, D. M. (2019). Leadership, uncertainty and risk: How leaders influence teachers. *Journal of Professional Capital and Community.* Advance online publication. Retrieved from https://doi.org/10.1108/JPCC-02-2019-0002

Twyford, K., Le Fevre, D., & Timperley, H. S. (2017). The influence of risk and uncertainty on teachers' responses to a professional learning and development initiative. *Journal of Professional Capital and Community, 2*(2), 86–100.

Vygotsky, L. S. (1978). *Mind in society: The development of higher psychological processes.* Cambridge, MA: Harvard University Press.

Websites

Implicit Association Test (IAT)
https://implicit.harvard.edu/implicit/

Your Story, Our Journey
www.yourstoryourjourney.net

www.ingramcontent.com/pod-product-compliance
Lightning Source LLC
Chambersburg PA
CBHW061126070526
44584CB00033B/4237